ON THE OTHER SIDE

ON THE OTHER SIDE

**The Report of the
Evangelical Alliance's
Commission on Evangelism**

SCRIPTURE UNION
5 Wigmore Street, London, W.1.

First published 1968

SBN 85421 199 3

PRINTED AND BOUND IN GREAT BRITAIN BY
HAZELL WATSON AND VINEY LTD
AYLESBURY, BUCKS

CONTENTS

Chapter Two: The Bible Says...
The Report of the Theological Group

7

MEMBERSHIP OF COMMISSION

Working Group

The Rev. Philip Crowe, M.A. Latimer House, Editorial Director, Church of England Newspaper.

The Rev. Ron. E. Davies, B.D., M.Th. Tutor, All Nations Missionary College, Ware, Herts.*

The Rev. Bryan E. Gilbert, B.D. Minister, Earls Hall Baptist Church, Southend-on-Sea.

The Rev. John Lancaster, Minister, Elim Church, Eastbourne.

Miss Anne Long, B.A., B.D. Tutor, Mount Hermon Missionary Training College.

The Rev. J. David Pawson, M.A., B.Sc. Minister, Guildford Baptist Church (Chairman).

Miss Anne Quilliam, B.A. Assistant Secretary, CPAS Women's Action.

The Rev. H. E. Roberts, Vicar of St. James the Less, Bethnal Green and St. Mark, Victoria Park, Bow.

The Rev. A. Morgan Derham, General Secretary, Evangelical Alliance.

Miss Ruth Henshall (Secretary).

* Mr. Davies ceased to be an active member because of new commitments undertaken in 1967.

Reference Group

The Rev. L. Roy Barker, M.A. Vicar, St. Mary's, Upton, Wirral, Cheshire.

The Rev. John L. Bird. Minister, Richmond Baptist Church.

Mr. H. F. Deeks. Shop Steward.

Mr. Martin Higginbottom. Director, Outreach to Industry.

9

Dr. James M. Houston, M.A., B.Sc., D.Phil. Fellow and Bursar of Hertford College, Oxford; Lecturer in Geography at Oxford University.

The Rev. R. Peter Johnston, M.A. Vicar, St. Mary's Islington.

The Hon. C. W. Joynson-Hicks. Solicitor. Chairman, Pathfinders.

Mrs. Joynson-Hicks. Housewife.

The Rev. Derek J. Prime, M.A., S.Th. Minister, Lansdowne Evangelical Free Church.

The Rev. Gavin H. Reid, B.A. Editorial Secretary, Church Pastoral-Aid Society.

Mr. Leith Samuel, B.A. Minister, Above Bar Church, Southampton.

The Rev. David Sheppard, M.A. Warden, Mayflower Family Centre, Canning Town, London, E.16.

Mr. Don Summers, Evangelist.

Mr. Jack F. Wallace, LL.B. Solicitor.

Dr. Verna Wright, M.B., Ch.B., M.D., M.R.C.P. Senior Lecturer in Medicine and Consultant Physician in Rheumatology to the United Leeds Hospitals and the Leeds Regional Hospital Board. Chairman, NYLC, Leeds.

Mr. John A. Webb, Architect. Council Member, Musical Gospel Outreach.

Advisers

Mr. Wm. E. Andersen. Lecturer in Educational Psychology, Sydney University, Australia.

Mr. David Longley, Formerly Assistant Pastor, Above Bar Church, Southampton – now with Wycliffe Bible Translators, Ghana.

Group of Statistical and Computer Advisers

Dr. David Shoesmith, Mr. Peter Brierley, Dr. Colin Day, and others.

The 1966 National Assembly of Evangelicals, sponsored by the Evangelical Alliance, passed a resolution worded as follows:

'In view of the urgent spiritual need of the nation, this Assembly –

(a) Dedicates itself anew to the task of Evangelism, recognizing its need for a Scriptural experience of the direction and dynamic of the Holy Spirit.

(b) Calls for the setting up of a Commission on Evangelism, which will prayerfully consider and recommend the best means of reaching the unchurched masses at national, local and personal levels, bearing in mind the need to co-ordinate existing endeavours where possible and specifically to promote a new emphasis on personal evangelism.'

The Council of the Alliance readily agreed to do this, and the primary responsibility was given to the General Secretary, acting in consultation with his colleagues. It was clear that such a Commission would have to consist of a small group which could develop a close understanding; at the same time, a larger body would have to be referred to, in order to give the Commission adequate breadth of vision and understanding of different situations.

In making suggestions for the membership of the Commission proper we kept in mind the need to have men and women of the younger generation; as it turned out, all the members of the Working Group were under forty at the time of their appointment. Denominationally they represent a wide coverage, roughly corresponding to the E.A.'s constituency. Functionally they include ministers, a minister-evangelist, Bible college staff and staff members of evangelical societies.

The larger reference body was, as can be seen from the list of members, a much more representative group, denominationally, functionally and geographically.

The Commission's work was done at two levels. The smaller Working Group operated in teams of two on the different sections, carrying out the 'field' work and preparing drafts. The group met together at monthly intervals. The larger 'Reference' body met four times – twice in London for one-day meetings, and twice in longer, residential conferences at Chalfont St. Peter – to advise the Working Group and consider their drafts.

The Report is therefore the work of the smaller Group, which takes responsibility for its findings and recommendations; but it also represents substantially the views of the Reference body, which guided and commented upon their work at each stage.

The Chairman took a close interest in the work of the different sections, and himself drafted the first outline of the final section. All the drafts were given final revision, and collated, by the General Secretary and the Editorial Secretary of the Evangelical Alliance, in consultation with Mr. Pawson.

Introduction

ON THE OTHER SIDE

The title is deliberately chosen to say little to those who only glance at the cover and contents of our Report. It will say a lot more to those who read, mark, learn and inwardly digest these pages. The phrase comes from the New Testament, of course, and four passages pin-point the thrust of our findings.

They passed by on the other side (Luke 10). Who did? A priest and a levite, ministers within God's people. Why did they do it? The story does not say. Hurrying to or from some important meetings at the temple, they got as far away from a man's real need as they could. Maybe they could have supported their action from Scripture. (Contact with a corpse was defiling.) The fact remained that they lacked love. Their failure was only accentuated by the compassionate action of someone outside the people of God.

They came to the other side (Mark 5). Who did? Twelve disciples at the invitation of Jesus. It meant leaving behind an interested congregation. It meant facing a dangerous voyage. It meant meeting a demented man and directly confronting the supernatural powers of evil. It meant a move from known Jewish territory to unknown Gentile territory. It meant misunderstanding, suspicion and antagonism. It was part of their training to be fishers of men.

They cast their nets on the other side (John 21). Who did? Seven experienced fishermen, on the advice of a carpenter. It was not the usual time or place; a change of strategy was

13

involved. They were already exhausted after trying every-thing they knew. Yet they did it and found success.

They found Him on the other side (John 6). Who did? The hungry crowd who wanted more. True, they were more interested in physical things than spiritual. True, they would rather see His miracles than hear His message. True, they would lose interest in Him very quickly, but they were seek-ing Jesus and they were prepared to go on looking for Him until they found Him.

This Report assumes that effective evangelism depends on the number of Christians who really care for others, who are prepared to enter into their world, who are willing to alter traditional methods, and who believe that people will be in-terested in the Lord in spite of their attitude to the Church. The fundamental plea of this Commission may be summed up in these words:

'Let us go across to the other side' (Mark 4.35).

Chapter One

THROUGH THE LOOKING GLASS

The Report of the Sociological Group

1. BRITAIN TODAY

Once again Britain is in the melting-pot. In the mid-nineteenth century the Industrial Revolution forced many to recognize that new means must bring new ways, new ways new ideals, and new ideals must bring changes in our whole social structure. Now, a hundred years later, we find ourselves caught up in another social revolution which is gathering momentum at a speed proportionately faster and more breathtaking than the earlier one. We may have become wise to some of the errors made by the Church in the nineteenth century, but must we wait another century before reaching an objective estimate of our present times? Are we intent upon understanding and assessing our society, in order to shape our Christian strategy accordingly? If not, the gulf to be bridged will be proportionately wider, the opportunities for correction probably fewer.

(a) Encouraging Features

Since the introduction of the 'Welfare State' in 1945, there have been general and widespread improvements in health, housing, provision for families, and care of the elderly. Whatever the pitfalls of the system, the overall benefits are obvious.

Likewise with the country's education programme, through the implementing of various Acts and Commissions, especially the 1944 Act, we have seen bold and imaginative steps forward. No longer are school lessons passive and dull – questions, activity and exploration abound, increased facilities and opportunities are available, and many more in a wide age-range can learn with enjoyment. Many Christians in other countries envy us our legislation concerning Religious Education lessons and school worship, and, generally speaking, this provision for children to gain religious knowledge and spiritual insights during their school days is widely appreciated by their parents. In a recent survey made amongst parents in North East England, it emerged that 85% of the sample questioned were agreed about the importance for all children in state schools of the Religious Education and worship required by law. In addition, there is a very strong desire that schools should continue to provide religious instruction and daily worship even if not legally obliged to do so.[1]

When we look at the young people emerging from our education system there is also room for encouragement. Sir Edward Boyle wrote: 'It is a bad mistake to become too pre-occupied with the negative aspects of present-day morality – the so-called collapse of standards. I believe that there is a higher incidence of courage and thoughtfulness among young people today than ever before. Moral considerations weigh strongly with them, but must be related to situations and choices which have relevance in terms of their own experience'.[2] Ventures such as Voluntary Service Overseas, the Duke of Edinburgh's Award Scheme, and different community projects are growing fast, but they only affect a small proportion of the total youth of the country.

1. See Report of Survey by P. R. May and O. R. Johnston 'Parental Attitudes to Religious Education in State Schools'. *Durham Research Review* (March 1967).
2. 'The Permissive Society', *The Guardian* (Autumn 1967).

More generally, we could say that amongst young people today there is a basic honesty, frankness, sincerity, seriousness and a desire to discover what will satisfy. Many speak in terms of 'finding themselves', 'personal fullness', and 'maturity'.

(b) Discouraging Features

Yet it is very evident that there is also another side to the picture. Despite the benefits of the Welfare State, we have increasingly seen a breakdown of old patterns and sanctions, a breakdown which is exposing new social problems. Despite improvements in housing and provisions made for families, there are still approximately 41,000 divorces per year out of some 360,000 marriages – about one divorce for every nine marriages. It is also an ugly fact that one out of every six children born is conceived out of wedlock. The problem of crime is even more alarming. In 1899 for every million people there were some 3,000 indictable offences per annum. Today the figure has risen to about 18,000, a rise of nearly six times. In addition, 30% of all convicted criminals today are seventeen years of age or under. In London some 50% of housebreaking and burglary offenders are between the ages of 8 and 16 years. Such figures show something of the widespread breakdown in standards and rejection of stable moral laws. Moreover, whilst there is certainly more State provision now for the elderly, they are still regarded as 'social problems' rather than persons.

We do well to be grateful for all improvements in education, yet we need to exercise a serious sense of responsibility in considering the implications for us of a system where investigation, choice and even scepticism are encouraged. The cult of 'scientism' has affected most of us in this century, and our children are being brought up in an atmosphere where it is generally accepted that 'science has the answers'. Such thinking brings new challenges to teachers of Religious

17

Education particularly, and calls for a more thoughtful presentation of religious concepts than is often given in both day and Sunday schools. It would be wrong to be pessimistic about the good being done in education but we must also be wise regarding the outcome. Neither can we necessarily regard the present legislation for Religious Education and school worship as an inevitable safeguard, for in this matter Britain is unusual rather than usual and there is no reason why such legislation should not be rescinded – indeed, many, including some Christians, think it should be.

As for young people today, whilst we welcome their concern for honesty, frankness, and fulness of living, even when it does cut across accepted convention, they often show an alarming disdain for experience. Sir Edward Boyle, in the article already quoted, went on to say: 'One striking mark of such contemporary dissent is, surely, its militant disdain for restraint.' Some may well be honest, but it is often the honesty of open revolt. Student strikes in Universities and Colleges are now a frequent phenomenon. The Albemarle Report [3] investigated some of the causes of unrest amongst young people, as did a fairly recent sociological study of young people made by Mary Morse. [4] Many express unrest and dissatisfaction whilst others speak openly of revolt. One of the 'prophets' of the pop generation wrote: 'I think England is more right for a youth revolution than America is, and I think the effect on British society will end up being more far-reaching, because the majority of British kids are treated in much the same way as the Americans treat the American Negro . . . If ever there's a situation right for a youth revolution, it's Britain today.' [5] There is evidence that those born since the war have a language and attitude of mind bred in a technological and electronic age so different

3. Albemarle Report. H.M.S.O.
4. Mary Morse: *The Unattached* (Penguin).
5. Joe Boyd: *Melody Maker* (October 28th, 1967).

from that of earlier generations that there are whole areas of life in which there is no shared experience at all.

(c) A Mirror to the Melting-Pot

The social revolution we face is not limited to one age-group or social group. We have selected some first-hand statements to illustrate something of this melting-pot as we see it. In the following chapter we hope to penetrate and understand some of the attitudes and thinking underlying such statements.

Marriage is hotly under fire today, and it was hardly surprising, though disturbing, to see the whole of an *Observer* Colour Supplement entitled 'Are we the last married generation?' and given up to a 'modern appraisal' of marriage. The Leader read: 'Are we the last married generation? . . . It is nothing new to find marriage ignored or regarded as only one of a number of alternatives . . . Is the ideal of "for better or for worse" relevant for very much longer?'[6] To treat a divine ordinance as optional would shock many, yet it is only to be expected in such a fluid situation as we find ourselves in. Consequently it is hardly surprising when Mary Quant, writing on the married woman,[7] bluntly declares: 'Now that there is the pill, women are the sex in charge. They, and they only, can decide to conceive.' This, again, is understandable rather than a shock in the context of today's humanistic thinking. Concerning *Man*, Dr. Edmund Leach can declare: 'Men have become like gods. Isn't it about time that we understood our divinity? Science offers us total mastery over our environment and over our destiny, yet instead of rejoicing we feel deeply afraid. Why should this be?'[8] In ironic contrast we quote a newspaper report on *Violence*: 'In 1965 one British city, Birmingham, suffered

6. *Observer*, Colour Supplement Leader (September 17th, 1967).
7. Mary Quant: 'The Permissive Society', *The Guardian* (November 1967).
8. Dr. Edmund Leach, Reith Lecture (November 12th, 1967).

19

damage to public property through vandalism at the rate of £1,000 a week. The figures for 1966 were little different. In January of this year, the Corporation . . . launched a "Stop Vandalism Week" to bring home to the community the seriousness of the problem.'[9]

Concerning *Industry,* we are constantly being reminded that we are hovering near the brink of crisis. Professor Niblett of London University has said: 'England is very much on the self-defensive. Employer and employees don't want to take risks. Defensiveness and drift go together and this typifies many of England's moral problems at present.'[10] A similar position of uneasy flux was pointed out when we spoke to Mr. D. Anderson, M.P., about *Politics*: 'Morale is low because Britain is looking for a rôle to take over instead of the old imperialistic position, because of the industrial malaise and economic problems. Hence many large and often pessimistic questions arise in people's minds – "Where do we go from here?" '[11] Richard Hoggart, writing for *The Guardian* on *Sociological Needs* also reflects the current instability: 'Many traditional values are being shaken, and we haven't much idea which need to be discarded, which modified, and which held on to.'[12] We are constantly being faced with the problem of values through the medium of TV. Mr. Penry Jones said to us: 'The problem for society with TV is its incorporation within the home setting and its representation of standards formerly not met, at any rate in the home.'[13] David Tribe, President of the National Secular Society, also said to us, 'Television has changed us all'.

Finally, it almost goes without saying that attitudes to

9. *The Guardian* (November 15th, 1967).
10. Prof. W. R. Niblett, Dean, Institute of Education, University of London.
11. Mr. D. Anderson, M.P. (October 24th, 1967).
12. Richard Hoggart, Director, Centre of Contemporary Cultural Studies, University of Birmingham. 'The Permissive Society', the *Guardian* (October 1967).
13. Penry Jones, Head of Religious Broadcasting, B.B.C.

Authority are also in the melting-pot. Mick Jagger, of the Rolling Stones, spoke on this at his trial in 1967: 'It's when authority won't allow something that I dig in. I'm against anything that interferes with individual freedom. As a non-conformist I won't accept what other people say is right. And there are hundreds like me, thousands.' Mr. W. Harford Thomas, Deputy Editor of *The Guardian*, commented: 'We must take notice of the upsurge of pop-groups with their anti-establishment, anti-authoritarian thinking. They are significant.'

Such comment, though far from exhaustive, at least covers a certain representation of contemporary opinion, and shows the significance of the 'melting-pot' figure of speech.

(d) Individualism and Fragmentation

Such ferment must affect the basic structures of society, and two key words which might describe the changes taking place are *Individualism* and *Fragmentation*. The thing which impressed the advertising executive responsible for the recent Salvation Army Campaign – 'FOR GOD'S SAKE, CARE' – during the planning stages, and which partly inspired its theme, was the isolation and lack of concern of people for each other. 'People have become isolated units within themselves,' he said. In several interviews we conducted, people suggested that it takes a war or a disaster of similar magnitude to give our nation identity and a sense of solidarity, and since the last war we have drifted further and further into individualism. Individualism becomes isolation for many who in new urban developments are stacked in compartments, upwards in tower blocks or horizontally behind the privacy of privet hedges. Entertainment is piped to the home, and life demands only a minimum of encounter with any other person.

The resultant outworking of Individualism within the basic groupings of society is Fragmentation. There is a breaking-up process at work leading to the destruction of traditional patterns. At one end of the scale national solidarity is weakening. Patriotism is hardly a serious matter. And if patriotism is a joke, at the other end of the scale of traditional groupings the family is certainly also under attack. Some maintain that youthful disorder is a symptom of the breakdown of family life. Edmund Leach argues: 'Nearly all the large-scale social changes which have taken place over the past century have been of a kind that should have brought children closer to their parents rather than the other way about . . . But in practice it seems to work out the other way: the adults are now inclined to treat teenagers as alienated ruffians – and not wholly without cause'. He continues: 'Perhaps it is the family itself that needs to be changed, rather than the parents. Far from being the basis of the good society, the family, with its narow privacy and tawdry secrets, is the source of all our discontents.'[14] Our own experience of family life may cause us to agree or disagree with this statement. Even if we disagree completely, yet we are all aware of a general loosening of the restraints which have maintained the family as a basic unit in our society. Whether our experience is closer to the anthropology of Dr. Leach or to the Colour Supplement type of debate on marriage as a 'working arrangement', or whether we have suffered the consequences of a broken home, we know that the family is no longer regarded as sancrosanct. The foundations of society as we have known it are fragmenting.

In 1941 Lord Salisbury predicted: 'More than death, wounds or destruction, I dread the moral desert that lies ahead. . . This war is going to destroy the moral sense of the nations. Values that it has taken generations to establish will be smashed. I do not mean the political and economic changes that are bound to come. They may be

14. Reith Lecture (November 26th, 1967).

good for us all – I cannot say. But the smashing of absolute standards of morality that you and I believe in, the denial of the truths of the spirit, the elevation of man's mind and body in place of God – these are things out of which nothing but darkness and decay can come, and these are the things that I see before us.' The truth of his words seems increasingly self-evident. We would not deny that there are encouraging features in contemporary society – more than we have had space to mention – but, at the same time, it is clear that we are passing through turbulent and alarming days. To return to our original metaphor, England is in the melting-pot.

2. BRITISH SOCIETY AND CULTURE

So far we have simply tried to hold a mirror to England in the mid-twentieth century to give a quick impression of what we have observed, read, and heard in our Commission investigations. We have made little attempt to analyse the scene, in the hope that it might speak for itself. However, in this chapter, we intend not so much to observe as to ask ourselves: what are some of the chief influences that have made for our present situation? If we are in the midst of a social revolution, what kind of thinking has brought this about, and why? People are questioning past assumptions and traditional values, not always to cast them out as useless but to establish what they consider to be valid and satisfying for today, both for community and individual. Within the scope of this Report we can be neither detailed nor comprehensive; we have therefore selected three areas for investigation: Young People and Education, Urbanization, and Mass Media.

In studying these areas, we have become very much aware of the new philosophies which owe their origin to the 'Enlightenment' of the eighteenth century. On one side, we now grapple with empiricism. Rejecting the supernatural, and insisting on verification, this view is essentially optimistic and is the basis for secularised humanism. On the other side, we are confronted with existentialism. Separating faith and reason, this view is essentially pessimistic about the meaning of life. Both philosophies have invaded the territory of Christian belief, producing such syntheses as Neo-orthodoxy and the more radical New Theology.

We must be fully informed about the intellectual strongholds of modern man and equipped with an apologetic able to exploit their weakness. Within the compass of this Report we are not able to do more than urge Evangelicals to study such investigations of this field as those of Dr. Francis Schaeffer (page 51, footnote 34, gives titles).

(a) Young People and Education

A. *General Impressions*

In our first chapter we mentioned some of the encouraging characteristics of young people today – a spirit of enterprise, a keen sense of social justice and, despite the prevalent permissive spirit, a genuine desire for honesty, sincerity, and frankness. The demands for education and college places are greater than ever, and many students speak of their desire to 'find themselves', to enjoy 'fulness of living'. Older people may sense an attitude of defiance amongst the young, but this is often only a cover-up for a determination to think constructively and clearly. Yet, if we are fair and try to assess the whole scene, we can well understand the fearfulness and pessimism of some parents and grandparents as they watch the acceleration of cults amongst young people, successively more weird and wonderful. Whether or not a 'youth revolution' is imminent, the present state of instability, flux, and rebellion would prove an effective seed-bed for one. Idealism is an encouraging characteristic in any young person, but in our contemporary society it often sours into cynicism – and is this surprising, when the world is what it is? Yet if these negative, anti-social characteristics alarm us, surely the answer is not simply to object and criticize but rather to seek to understand, penetrate, and communicate.

With any age-group or social grouping, we can only understand the part in its relation to the whole. Generally a young person will reflect within himself the situation outside himself. Thus, in today's permissive atmosphere, there is amongst young people a fairly solid resistance to tradition which, in this country, tends to include religion and its trappings – its distinctive buildings, forms of service, modes of dress and prohibitions. Perhaps now, more than at any other time in history, the Church is in danger of substituting traditions for the commandments of God. We must constantly be recognizing both the dangers and the challenges of distinguishing between the genuine historic Christian faith and traditionalism. Pharisaism is most speedily detected by young people who are trained in schools and colleges today to ask questions, test validity, and reject anything that seems unreal or impracticable. So when so many declare themselves to be Anti-Establishment, Anti-Government, Anti-Church, Anti-Dogma, they are not simply saying 'We don't and won't believe all this!' but rather, 'We won't believe until we have worked these things out for ourselves.' Similarly with leisure and affluence, young people want them on their own terms rather than organized by their elders in a traditional, middle-class way. They don't want to be fenced within secure situations, but rather to discover their own security. Risk, sex, untidiness – even violence – must not be shut out. 'These are real,' they say, 'and we're going to look at them.' Hence the re-introduction of such elements into teenage culture.

B. Education Today

If these are some of the general impressions given by some (not all) young people today, we ought to try and gain some insight into the educational system that seeks to guide and formulate their thinking. Schools are intimately related to the society within which they function. John Vaizey [15] writes: 'Schools both affect and mirror the quality of society.' Education is important, he maintains, 'to help children, to give them better lives, to improve the society in which we live.' Schools must be 'geared to the world we live in, preparing people for life and change'. Of course, school is only one of several formative influences in a child's life, yet increasingly this country is adopting policies of 'total education', providing ground for training in social relationships, vocational and psychological counselling, extra-curricula activities and holiday courses. Athough examination requirements still govern many secondary school timetables, so that education is often still geared to achievement, a more recent trend is to produce a pattern aiming at self-fulfilment and all-round development. No longer is it just the prospective scholar or white-collar worker who is encouraged, but people in most kinds of work and social groupings. More comprehensive schools will, it is hoped, bring increased equality of opportunity, more scope for social cohesion and better community training.

Primary education is very different today from what it was twenty years ago. A modern Primary School, far from being a passive scene where children sit still at their desks, is a hive of activity. Teaching is largely carried out by the children's own discovery and participation and they are encouraged to ask the questions 'Why?' or 'How?' as often as possible. This is surely a good and necessary trend in an age when we are increasingly exposed to second-hand in-

15. John Vaizey: *Education for Tomorrow* (Pelican).

fluences through mass media. Most of our learning in the past has been rational, forgetting intuitive and emotional factors. With increased insight into personality development, educationists are realizing that rational thinking and development cannot take place without accompanying intuitive and emotional involvement.

In *Secondary education*, because of examination requirements, we are still seeing some tension between a specialization which can lead to a fragmentary view of life, and a more integrated, inter-related teaching aimed at 'wholeness' of thinking. Partly as a reflection of the current philosophical and theological climate, we see an interesting ambivalence between attitudes expressed by science and arts sixth-formers. The sixth-form scientist has great confidence in man, his mind and his ability, whereas the arts student is often far more defensive and pessimistic, asking more basic questions about life, questions about which science says little or nothing. Yet, whatever their training, in whatever kind of secondary school and however partial their interpretation of life, teenagers are undoubtedly more internationally minded and politically intelligent than formerly, anxious to know where they are going, many of them very honest and sensitive to any form of hypocrisy. At almost every stage of their secondary education, dialogue, discussion, and frank questioning are encouraged so that young people become used to challenging authority, posing their queries and demanding honest interchange. This point is worth pondering for it contrasts strongly with much of our Church teaching where, as the Rev. J. R. W. Stott puts it: 'most preachers place themselves six feet above contradiction.' [16] There is much positive evidence in Scripture to suggest that dialogue is a right and good teaching method which could be used far more widely in our churches. If young people are asking questions, is this to be construed as wrong and difficult, or

16. J. R. W. Stott: *The Preacher's Portrait* (I.V.F.).

wonderful? But to present scriptural truth in this way is exacting, demanding both a firm hold on the Scriptures and also a resilience in listening to new questions and new ways of thinking.

Higher Education is mushrooming, and will continue to do so in the next few years, at a breath-taking rate. The student population in 1960 was *c.* 170,000; in 1970, it is estimated by the Robbins Report, figures will have doubled to *c.* 340,000, or some 15% of that age group. New Universities, Colleges, and Technical Colleges are appearing and, again, reflect much of the spirit of the age. Permissiveness is more evident in some than others, though many students are genuinely concerned about this. They regard freedom of speech, thought, and action as their right, whether they are prepared to use it or not. Protests, and even strikes, over matters for concern both in and outside the college are quite common now and are surely symptomatic of a change in the students' attitudes towards their rights and responsibilities.

Religion, too, is open to speculation and debate. One question posed by Peter Morris in a survey of Cambridge, Leeds, and Southampton Universities, was 'What preoccupies student debates and conversations?' [17] His findings showed that 'Just over one quarter of students said their last discussion had concerned religion, the existence of God, doctrinal differences, the personality of Christ'. Other subjects discussed in descending order of popularity next to religion were politics/current affairs, personal relationships and sex, education, philosophy. The Universities' Secretary of the Inter-Varsity Fellowship told us that generally the questions asked by students are very basic ones, *e.g.*, 'Who *is* God?', 'What's He like?' He maintained that there is also much need and scope for 'pre-evangelism' such as

17. Peter Morris: *The Experience of Higher Education; a survey of Cambridge, Leeds and Southampton Universities.*

pushing agnosticism to its logical conclusions in order to show that the system breaks down or has no pragmatic value. Often it is necessary to work back before working forwards, for many students have not yet worked out the logicality and tenability of their thinking. In the present student situation, no previous Christian knowledge can necessarily be assumed; there is less nominalism and a correspondingly more clear-cut missionary situation.

What is the attitude of young Christians entering into this situation in the Universities? Broadly speaking there seem to be two. Christian students going up with a good, positive, carefully considered Christian background of teaching are articulate and confident in witness, with a genuine concern for non-Christians. On the other hand, those going up from insular church backgrounds are often on the defensive, fearful, inhibited and negative, more often creating an inward-looking ghetto than an outward-looking, lively fellowship, and either ignoring or finding themselves unable to cope with the questions of other students. Is this a reflection of the teaching and quality of life experienced in some local churches from whose ranks students move out to further education? If so, it is small wonder that some graduates find it hard to settle back into insular local churches, after enjoying the freedom of interchange within a college setting.

Probably something more specific should be said now about *Religious Education* in this country. Religious Education is the one subject, that must, by law, appear on the school timetable. Religious worship has also been legislated for – a fact which Christians in other countries sometimes envy. Currently, R.E. is in the news, and also in the melting-pot. Research into the religious concepts of children and young people is causing many Education Authorities to revise teaching syllabuses; some denominational Sunday school departments are following on, giving less time and space to specific Bible teaching and substituting more general 'life themes' with religious significance. Not surprisingly, many Evangelicals are feeling defensive and wary, disregarding the points at which we can learn from such research and hard thinking. It is unlikely that R.E. and religious worship will suddenly disappear from our schools, but we should feel the fact that an increasing number of people would like it to.

Why is R.E. taught? Opinions are manifold. Surely the purpose of it is not to proselytize – even though it is always good to hear of individuals coming into new personal convictions through the agency of R.E. lessons. But, to quote P. R. May and O. R. Johnston: 'To blur the functions of church and school, or preacher and teacher, is to do a grave disservice to both institutions. In a democratic society, unless the vast majority of citizens profess the Christian faith *and* have specifically entrusted the work of child evangelism to the schools, evangelism is not the function of religious education.' [18] Neither is it our aim, as Christian teachers, to indoctrinate or encourage hypocritical conformity. Rather it is the aim of R.E. to give clear insights into both the contents and the ethos of the Christian faith, its historicity, its literature, and its morality. Young people cannot pronounce upon what they are ignorant of. (Of course, they often do, but this is often just as much a reflection of poor teaching as of biased viewpoints.) They must be given the opportunity to be confronted with what the Bible says and how it has influenced much of our national thinking and culture. On the basis of such teaching, young people will then be in a position to discuss, debate, and accept or reject the Christian faith.

Such teaching requires well-trained, informed teachers who are not afraid to break away from traditional ap-

18. P. R. May and O. R. Johnston: *Religion in our Schools* (Hodder & Stoughton).

proaches on the subject and who are open to any questions. It has often been assumed that 'anyone' can teach R.E., but we are now seeing some of the results of dull, unimaginative, authoritarian, defensive teaching. Young people are being taught to question, and can apply their questions to any area of life and thought in their search for satisfactory answers. In the light of current thinking, it is vital that teachers, youth leaders and Sunday school teachers keep informed on what is being said about R.E., understand and sift the methods being adopted, and remain open, fair and non-authoritarian in their approach. Parents, too, must realize their responsibility. The Editor of *The Christian* wrote: 'If Christian parents take no interest in parent-teacher gatherings, in the workings of the local education authority, and in parliamentary discussion and legislation on educational matters, they may soon and sharply find that the forces of irreligion have not lost *their* zeal.'[19]

Finally, the churches must see their part in this. It is their job to evangelize and teach those young people who will eventually become teachers of Religious Education. They must set the example of better and more up-to-date teaching of religion in Sunday school and youth groups. 'Ultimately the educational health of our schools will depend upon the spiritual health of our churches. And the spiritual health of our churches depends in the last resort upon the faithfulness of individual Christians and the preaching and teaching of the Word of God.' [20]

C. The Challenge

In the face of current trends in education, we would suggest the following as points of challenge for Christian churches, youth leaders, teachers and others working amongst children and young people:

19. Editorial, *The Christian* (February 23rd, 1968).
20. P. R. May and O. R. Johnston: *Religion in our Schools*.

1. In a recent enquiry carried out amongst some 200 Sixth Formers who claimed to be Christians, one question invited their criticisms of the Church. The answers are noted here in order of importance:
   (a) too self-contained, does not communicate to non-Christians.
   (b) too organized, not enough flexibility.
   (c) no encouragement to young people.
   (d) should concentrate on agreement between denominations, not differences.
   (e) no 'togetherness'; distance between young and old.
   (f) 'lifeless', 'pompous', 'cold', 'cliquish', 'stuffy', 'holy huddle'.

   Another question asked how sermons could be made more helpful. Answers included the following points:
   (a) relevant topics – suggestions from the congregation.
   (b) illustrate from everyday life.
   (c) consider the needs and problems of young people.
   (d) sermons to be discussed.
   (e) use meaningful language.

   These comments come from church-going young people and should be noted as an honest reflection of what they feel.

2. We must therefore learn to communicate our faith at all levels in different social groups and age groups, in an open youth club if we work there, or with six-year-olds in a day school. This will mean understanding the ways in which children and young people think and the twentieth-century cultural factors influencing them. It will mean discovering an honesty, openness, and meaningfulness in informal discussion which, in turn, will demand our being informed about what we believe. Our manner will need to be authoritative without becoming authoritarian, and in our own thinking we must be willing to distinguish between the true historical Christian faith and traditional

trimmings and prejudices. A letter published in *The Guardian* contained this statement: 'A good number of the young people I meet have rejected Christianity, not because of a conscious decision of will taken after weighing up both sides, but as a result of prejudices (due to the general climate of opinion) which close their mind to anything religious, deeming it not worthy even of consideration.'

3. Those of us working amongst young people must be constantly aware of new methods in education, teaching aids and current talking points.

4. Christian parents should observe their responsibility to keep informed about their children's schools and what is being taught. It is irresponsible to criticize the way R.E. is being taught and yet never attend a Parent-Teacher Association meeting or help supplement the school syllabus by informed discussion and conversation in the home.

(b) Urbanization

The modern world is an urban world. In England over 80% of the population lives in towns and cities. Indeed, the whole of the Western world is urbanized in its mode of life, even if a minority still inhabit the countryside. There is also now an unprecedented urban growth in the developing countries, creating radical social and economic changes within them. In 1850, 2·4% of the world's population lived in towns with over 20,000 inhabitants; in 1950 the percentage was 20·9 and it is estimated it will have risen to 45 in the year 2000, and even 90% in A.D. 2050. Although regionally diverse in its magnitude and relative size, urbanization – the process by which cities grow – is now a universal phenomenon. In the last few years Christians have become aware that the urban trends challenge church strategy.

Although cities have existed for several thousand years,

33

the whole basis of city growth has been revolutionized by industrialization. More recent urbanized landscapes have made the geographical patterns of parishes and the distribution of churches archaic.

Social historians have clearly demonstrated that the rise of the cities has been concomitant with the decline of religion.[21] In the first place, this has been the consequence of the sheer size of the new urban communities compared with the medieval villages. It is well established that the larger the city, the lower has been the proportion of church-goers. In a large urban community many more unchurched people get overlooked, and anonymity is generally more common.

A second consequence of urban growth with industrialization has been the destruction of the older forms of community with their simplicity of social structure. In place of a more homogeneous life where religion drew people together by its universal values, differing social classes tended to promote different aspirations. These were expressed in differing religious forms, with a tendency for the working classes to be less interested in religious values than the middle classes.

The impact of industrialization on modern city growth has had a third and most significant consequence on religious life. It has provided not only technical possibilities for further physical growth, but also a style of outlook that is increasingly autonomous and self-contained. This provides the ethos of secularization, whereby modern man feels liberated from religious and metaphysical controls, turning his attention from other worlds to this one. Both urbanization and secularization share three main characteristics: 1, reliance upon science and technology; 2, rationalized organization; and 3, the pragmatic spirit (that is, a concentration upon practical and material questions). Thus the

21. e.g. *Secularization and Moral Change*, by Alasdair McIntyre (O.U.P.).

physical processes of urbanization (by which cities grow) are paralleled by mental processes (by which society is being transformed in its outlook). Two prevailing outlooks are those of scientism and pragmatism. Scientism says that science is the only valid source of knowledge; and pragmatism argues that one should not indulge in those border-line questions or metaphysical problems that have no immediate concern with practical and material affairs. Life is thus looked at as a set of problems to be solved in a scientific spirit and not as a realm of unfathomable mystery.

The social consequences of city growth have been the intensification of anonymity, of social mobility, and of profanity. From a web of innumerable relationships the city-dweller chooses his close friends and treats the rest rather impersonally. There is a clear separation of private and public life. Loneliness and a loss of selfhood in urban anonymity are consequences of the city life. These all make the Christian doctrine of the Body of Christ a more elusive and more sophisticated concept.

The second consequence is that in a dynamic and expanding society, flexibility and the demands of employment promote mobility. And the mobile person is less likely to idolize the *status quo*; he is open to change with himself as well as with his society. Worshipping the cult of contemporaneity makes the mobile person in city life a formidable force for further revolution. This spirit is not a favourable one in which to propose the traditional values of Christian morality.

The third consequence of the city is its profanity. The great religious values of life are set aside to be replaced by more functional and pragmatic values. In such an ethos, religious belief has no longer the authority it once had. Rather the mood of the technical age is one of the this-worldly and the here-and-now.

City life is now altering also the concepts of work and

35

leisure. There is, firstly, the separation of work from residence. There is little work done now in the home, and with many more members of a family at work paternalism has virtually disappeared.

Secondly, organization man is here to stay. Bureaucratic institutions are now an inevitable feature of the modern city, in order to handle the growing complexities of technological advances and global business.

Thirdly, with automation, work no longer requires the same sense of vocation as once it did. Indeed, the view that work is 'virtuous' is itself being questioned. As automation increases so will the problem of the use of leisure become increasingly significant.

It is thus clear that the secular city is largely indifferent to Christian values and faith. What effective strategy of Christian mission is therefore required?

Perhaps, first of all, there is the need for Christian leaders to have a more coherent understanding of how the modern city operates and grows, and of the forces at work in its life. Many sections of urban population are untouched because their rôle in city life is not appreciated.

Secondly, there must be the ability to sense in the present some of the likely changes in the future, in order to anticipate tomorrow's problems. Planners have already published *Paris and London in the Year 2000*, but where is there a survey of Christian urban mission in the year 2000? How are we to plan for tomorrow's leisure in the church? How are we to utilize within the church the female manpower of 'liberated' housewives? How are we to promote the development of principles of cybernetics [22] that will preserve and sustain the dignity of man?

It is also obvious that the urban churches need to reshape their ministry in the light of changing city patterns. Instead of demarcating parish boundaries in spatial pat-

22. The study of systems of control and communication.

terns, the frontiers should be invisible and flexible. Instead of being inward-looking – towards a central church building – the local church needs to be more outward-looking, with church groups creating more cellular growth around home units, factory units, college units, etc.

Many more specialized ministries need to be promoted in such corporate structures as large stores, labour unions, universities, hospitals, etc. Much church life has centred around the terminals of life – among Sunday school children, University students, and the old. The churches must learn much more vitally to invade the midst of life, including life in the middle years, with its marked cynicism and sophistication. People must also be reached much more in the midst of their normal pursuits. Research, planning, and the co-ordinated promotion of Christian endeavours in strategic areas of city life need much more attention. There are the practical problems of Christian involvement in urban renewal, social reconstruction, and municipal politics. Christians must seriously accept urbanism and its challenges today.

(c) Mass Media

What influences people to change their minds in modern Britain? That there has been a substantial shift in emphasis on the part of those engaged in selling goods or ideas, over the past fifteen years, is undeniable. Door to door selling has declined; press advertising has changed its approach; television dominates the scene. When the experts set out to persuade us to change our brand of coffee, or our political allegiance, they go about it in a significantly different way today.

The changes arise partly from circumstances and partly from theory.

The changed circumstances include the advent of television as a mass medium of communication; the decline in the respectability of doorstep salesmanship; the increasing sophistication of the customers; and the reluctance of people to attend meetings and rallies.

The theoretical changes, mostly based on psychological studies, have meant a switch from 'hot' advertising (BUY THIS ⸺ IT'S THE BEST) to 'cool' advertising (WHAT IS A MUM?), and from straightforward proposition to subtle and elusive manipulation of human instincts, fears, and needs. Modern advertising seldom argues a case, but rather sets out to create dissatisfaction, awareness, or longing. Slowly the politicians have followed, offering not arguments (in their campaign publicity) but images, and setting out to offer answers to needs rather than questions.

Television

The influence of TV on British life can hardly be exaggerated. Radio is a powerful tool of persuasion, using only the ear for an entrance into man's mind; but television is many times more potent, for it also enters through the eye, that most impressionable of all the senses.

It is also a *mass* medium. With nearly 15 million TV licence holders, and an estimated potential TV audience very little smaller than the entire population of the UK, television wields an enormous influence both in breadth and depth. There is certainly no quicker or more effective way today to inculcate an idea than to put it across expertly on television. We live in a television culture, and it is dangerous blindness to ignore the medium.

The Press

At the same time Britain reads more newspapers (per head of the population) than any other country on earth. In recent years, too, the trend has been towards the quality papers, with their in-depth treatments and glossy magazine sections. It would seem that people get their capsule news and 'scoops' from radio and TV, but look increasingly to the Press for comment and interpretation.

Equally, the phenomenal market for 'pulp' paperback books and also the heavy borrowing of library books (mainly novels) represents another mass means of communication.

Cinema

Although the weekly average of admission to cinemas in the UK has dropped substantially over the last ten years, it is still over five million – that is, one adult in eight goes to the cinema once a week. Audiences are more discriminating since the advent of television, and it seems likely that people select the film they wish to see rather than simply attend out of habit. This means that films are still a highly effective medium for communicating ideas even in the 'television age'.

Mass media and the churches

The public reaction to religious TV (apart from the straight 'hymn-singing' programmes) is disturbingly negative. The programmes have small audiences, and seldom seem designed to do more than cater for an esoteric minority who wish to discuss sociological or ecclesiastical problems in a sophisticated vacuum. Few programmes in recent years have fired the imagination of the viewing public or disturbed their apathy about Christianity.

There would seem to be a serious shortage of men and women with a Christian commitment who are willing to dedicate themselves to radio and TV, raise their standards, and think imaginatively and radically about the task of presenting and applying the Christian Gospel in today's world.

The pioneer work of the Scripture Union's small 'Modern Communications Unit' has been highly commendable, and

Evangelicals should provide the means for it to expand its activities, as an urgent priority.

Similarly a meeting place for those engaged in creative and artistic work, who wish to express their Christian faith through drama, the novel, music or other media, is an urgent necessity. Those with the skills and gifts required must be able to experiment without fear of misunderstanding, and to discuss together the ways in which these media can be used in the cause of Christ. Christian producers, writers, composers and performers must be encouraged to persevere in the secular realm, where the real issues of the day are being fought out, rather than retire into evangelical ghettos to entertain the 'converted'.

Where the Press is concerned, the Church's chief concern should be for an accurate and just assessment of Christianity, both as philosophy and in action; and for an opportunity to use this medium to influence the tone of our national life and even the course of national events. This means, more than anything else, encouraging young and gifted Christians to enter the profession of journalism and make their way, on merit, up to its highest levels.

3. THE CHURCH IN ENGLAND

We must now look at the Church and ask ourselves how she is faring, hoping that the answers will help us see both the dangers and the opportunities that we face. We are not, at this point, offering a doctrinal statement about the Church – that can be found elsewhere in the Report. Rather, we are considering our place as Christians and church members in society, and also the way that non-Christians see the Church.

(a) Society's Influence upon the Church

Some Christians will be more aware of the situation that we have described than others. Our age, social group, education, job, and the newspapers we read will all have a share in determining our awareness of the atmosphere in which we live, but we are all affected by it, consciously or not. To be 'in the world but not of it' is a personal tension confronting every Christian, and it seems that there are two possible attitudes open to the Church in this situation. We spell them out as two extremes to be avoided: our path is knife-edged between being, on the one hand, dazzled and, on the other, depressed by the revolution going on around us.

It is all too easy for us to be dazzled: there is much in what we have described to attract, and Christ-given, abundant life means a greater enthusiasm and capacity for living. Is it any wonder that talk of revolution, new horizons, and new values should make the heart beat faster? Some Christians will go to extremes in an earnest desire to identify themselves with their non-Christian friends and colleagues. The danger in seeking identification with others in wrong ways is that our positive Christian identity is completely lost. We can even find ourselves witnessing to the wrong things, so that the Gospel is misunderstood. Imparting a distinctive flavour to society, which is one rôle of the Church, can only be done while we maintain our distinctiveness.[23]

But if there is a danger of being dazzled by our environment, we must admit that the greater and more general danger is to be depressed. Centuries of history warn us that at times of change the instinct of a large part of the Church is to be frightened by the challenge to its authority and to spring to an attitude of defence. In days when the Bible is under fire, this danger of depression is all the greater for Evangelicals who refer back to the distinctive authority of the written word of God; the more that authority is challenged, the greater our determination to defend it. But, un-

23. Matthew 5. 13.

41

less exercised in a positive spirit, determination can turn negatively defensive and our attitude can quickly become introverted and depressed. The individualism and fragmentation we have spoken of earlier can arise as easily in churches as in other groupings, and result in a lack of mutual trust, rifts between young and old, and uncertainty or division over authority and leadership.

(b) The Church's Impact upon Society

We are very conscious that it is in this area that we need the power and wisdom of God to see ourselves as we really are, and not to cover up reality with pious platitudes. The facts and figures collected by this Commission should give us some idea of the degree to which the Church has the ear of our nation, but on those rare occasions when we have that ear, does what we say make sense? God alone knows the answer to that question: are we ready to listen to Him?

Years of battling against enormous odds (numerically at least) are almost bound to breed in any local minister or congregation a defensive spirit reluctant to face facts which are almost too painful to bear. When faced with some area of society completely unaffected by the institutional Church, we can comfort ourselves with the knowledge that it is different for us, and if the church down the road is also having hard times, it is because they haven't our particular brand of truth. It is ironically easy to become more blind to a situation the deeper we get immersed in it.

Can God speak to the Church through non-Christians? We believe so, and often, during interviews for this Report, as we have listened to different voices we have heard God say: 'Face up to reality'.

The dramatist, John Osborne, wrote the following words in the early 1950s, but he was speaking for all angry young men then and now when he did so: 'During the past fifty years, the Church has repeatedly ducked every moral issue

42

that has been thrown at its head – poverty, unemployment, Fascism, war, South Africa, the H-bomb, and so on. It has lived in an atmosphere of calm, casual funk. It has not been entirely negative in its attitude. It has even managed to spread the gospel of funk. With its village quarrels about divorce and re-marriage, and its favourite topic – the re-imbursement of the clergy – its capacity for self-mockery has been unlimited.' [24] Even more recently, during our Commission interviews a young advertising executive said to us: 'I am a prospect for religion, but no one is selling it to me. The brand image of religion is meaningless. I'm not prepared to speak to the religious man because he's not prepared to speak my language. The brand image of the Church is meaningless, old-fashioned, opinionated, way behind the times, incomprehensible, irrelevant. What are your consumer benefits?'

The overwhelming impression of the picture we, as Christians, present to a non-Christian society is of a self-admiring, self-sufficient, introspective circle with some esoteric interest.

But it is not only non-Christians who will tell us this. Michael Green has written recently: 'If one of the uninitiated ventured close enough to listen, he could be pardoned for supposing that the Roman Catholics were primarily concerned with priestly defections, Vatican II, and birth control; the Anglo-Catholics would seem to be extremely anxious to ensure that the Methodist ministers got episcopally ordained; the Ecumenicals ardent for church mergers; the Radicals devoted to the New Theology and the New Morality; the Orthodox muttering about liturgy; the Pentecostals enthusing about speaking in tongues; and the Conservative Evangelicals going on about sin.' [25] Another minister said to us during interview: 'The Church is not

24. John Osborne: *Declaration*, p. 74.
25. Rev. Michael Green: *Man Alive* (I. V. F.).

43

failing to communicate. The Church is communicating precisely what it is – a casualty of the onrush of social change and the breakdown of authority. The failure is the Church's incapacity to listen to what is being communicated to it emotionally by society.' [26]

(c) A Closer Look at Social Groupings

It may seem irrelevant to some of our readers to speak in terms of the traditional class groups – upper, middle and working – especially when the dividing line between them is so uncertain, yet since these terms are still used amongst sociologists, we propose to use them, whilst recognizing that such groupings will not necessarily remain valid or meaningful indefinitely.

The traditional middle classes of English society are, by their very nature, self-perpetuating, a principle which in the past has worked for good and ill. The tradition of service associated with the professions and the Civil Service, for example, has been built upon this very fact, and much of the strength of English society in the past has been the direct result of the solid backbone given to our nation by this group. Within it the Church has had its most significant success. David Martin, in his very useful sociological survey of English religion,[27] describes how, following the Industrial Revolution, any significant impact made by the churches was in the midde classes. We see this equally today – more people from the middle classes attend churches than from the upper or working classes. Generally, the encouragements we have come from Grammar rather than from Secondary Modern schools, from Universities and Colleges rather than teenage gangs, from office Christian Unions rather than factory floors, from suburban churches

26. Rev. B. D. Reed, Director, Christian Teamwork Institute of Education.
27. David Martin: *A Sociology of English Religion* (Heinemann, 1967).

rather than industrial areas. Significant statistics bearing this out can be found in the ABC Gallup Poll's findings, *Television and Religion*.[28]

Not surprisingly, the liberating power of the Gospel and many positive Christian virtues – such as honesty, morality and the sanctity of work – have served to perpetuate this tendency for English Christianity to be expressed in a traditional, middle-class way. Thus, if a working-class man is converted, he is very likely to improve in his work and consequently move to a 'better' area where his children will have increased opportunity. In this way, he adds to the strength of the suburban church whilst weakening the already ailing church from which he came. It is perhaps partly for this reason that the Salvation Army and the Methodists, both of whom had their roots in the working classes, have become far more respectable and 'middle class' in recent years.

Today most churches recruit their ministry almost exclusively from the middle classes, and where a man does stray from some other background into the ranks of the ministry, he will be submitted to a training which almost certainly ensures that he will emerge with the attitudes and aptitudes to fit him for ministering to that same group. Thus the circle is almost complete, the Church drawn very largely from one section of society, ministering to itself. If the middle classes contained a large proportion of the population, this would not be such a matter for concern, but on most criteria this grouping accounts for only 10–20% of English society today.

The upper classes mostly live on their country estates. Those, however, who are in business often live in London during the week (Kensington, Chelsea, Mayfair, Belgravia)

28. ABC Gallup Poll: *Television and Religion* (University of London Press Ltd.).

but move elsewhere at weekends, probably to the home counties. They are not reached by local churches, largely because of the difference of social class between them and the clergy. Further difficulties may arise if they live and work in different places and also, particularly so far as the younger generation is concerned, because they are now less tied by convention than previously. Those few in the upper classes who are Christians and attached to local churches tend to live their faith without expressing it in words, both because it is not the done thing and because they have received little scriptural teaching. The principal method of reaching them with the Gospel is through personal friendship and by invitation to meetings organized by individuals (e.g. ladies' lunches, drawing-room or hotel meetings, dinner or coffee parties, Bible study groups). There is still considerable nominalism amongst the older, more traditional members of the upper classes, where religion is considered part of the respectable life. This is no longer true of those who are under say, forty, but concerning those over this age David Martin writes: 'It is God, the Supreme Being, rather than Christ the Saviour who forms the centre of worship: salvation is a word which belongs to the world of indecent enthusiasms and non-conformist fervour. . . . Duty is the obligation to lead: to run the Mothers' Union, the W.V.S., the Red Cross, and so on. To lead is to set an example to lesser breeds within the law, and this means that causal connections are believed to exist between elite behaviour and public morality in general. To be a prefect brings responsibility. It does not mean obtrusive piety, but it requires the performance of external rituals associated with one's station – maybe the reading of a lesson at Matins, attending a church parade, or else a care for the maintenance of the church's fabric because it is a symbol of national and perhaps familial continuity. Something would be gone from life if the church bells ceased to peal out over the peaceful shires.' [29]

The working classes still comprise the large part of English society. Estimates vary between 50% and 70%, amongst whom, Richard Hoggart writes, 'there is obviously a wide range of attitudes, and yet there is a centre at which a great number of people are represented.' [30] The term is still the best available to identify those manual workers who leave school at fifteen, read the *Daily Mirror*, live in local authority housing and stay away from church. Often they will send their children to Sunday school – they always have. David Martin writes of the 19th century: 'What degree of penetration occurred across these lines of class? Only the Sunday schools had any substantial success, and this would have occurred, it was said, even if the teachers had been "mild-mannered Buddhists", provided at least that they were white.' [31] But this only deepens the divide, since church is seen to be a place for children (and the elderly) and the children are only waiting for the day when they reach adult status and stay away like Mum and Dad. Sufficient to say that for most in this grouping the Church is an outdated irrelevance. We could all quote glorious exceptions, and thank God for them, but to a large extent working-class men and women regard the church as a place for 'them', not 'us'. Again, David Martin writes: "Hypocrisy" is the main epithet applied to those with church affiliation and it is almost universally maintained that those who do not attend church are as good as those who do. "You don't need to go to church to be a good Christian" is the nearest thing to a fundamental creed amongst working-class people. It may also be suggested that what goes on inside a church is out-of-date mumbo-jumbo. This puzzlement at liturgical complication is very genuine and particularly concerns the

29. D. Martin: *A Sociology of English Religion*, pp. 70–71.
30. R. H. Hoggart: *The Uses of Literacy* (1957, Pelican).
31. D. Martin: p. 27.

Church of England, in which every new ritual quirk or even reform devised by clergy only deepens the conviction that this is not designed for people "such as us".' [32]

It may seem strange to suggest similarities between the upper and working classes. Yet, concerning religion particularly, there are many points of contact. D. Martin writes: 'On two points the attitudes at the extremes of the social spectrum are identical: in equating religion with conduct, and in regarding one's beliefs as inappropriate for general discussion. Religion is equivalent to decency, and in the one case this may include attending church or running one of its organizations, and in the other case not. The universal reticence which goes with this emphasis on decency is partly a fear of ridicule, partly a wish to avoid any hint of contamination by religious fanaticism. The fear of ridicule is related to a masculine ethos which regards religious practice as appropriate for children and women, along perhaps with all the gentler arts. The English male is supposed to live up to an ideal of psychological opacity and cultural philistinism, and it may even be that his ideal is quite frequently attained.' He continues: 'It is not proper to discuss [religion] or subject it to intellectual elaboration. Dogma and theology in religion (as in politics) are symptoms of diseased intellectual enthusiasms which portend the ruin of the State.' [33]

If the Church is making as little impact on our society as we have suggested, can we see successful communication taking place in any sphere whereby people's thinking is being affected and moulded? It has become increasingly clear to us that there are voices influencing all social classes, though perhaps the older members of the middle classes with their more deeply-entrenched attitudes and conservative values are the most resistant towards them. We have

32. D. Martin, p. 69
33. D. Martin, p. 68.

48

had difficulty in describing these influential voices, for they represent a blend of several elements and often cut right across traditional class groupings. We would call them intellectuals if they did not include some of the show biz leaders, TV personalities, ad men and satirists. We would call them the swinging set if they did not make room for some of the writers, philosophers, actors, and artists who ought really to be called intellectuals. We therefore describe them as 'opinion formers'. It is unlikely that many of them would welcome the title, but in fact it describes their function. Many factors of the 1960s have bred a sensitivity to 'trends'. Permissiveness gives the boldness, affluence makes possible their pursuit, and mass media ensure that they are reported almost hourly. Whilst having the sympathy and attention of most young people, the opinion formers are not simply concerned to exploit teenage fashion and trends. In the nature of things they have the ear of the whole of society, but while the working classes are only too ready to listen (often unconsciously), the middle classes, particularly those who are older, resent their strident challenge to cherished values and authorities. This resentment is poignantly illustrated in some middle-class homes where younger members of the family heed the call of the opinion formers and bring this conflict right into the home, resulting sometimes in most painful clashes between the generations.

Needless to say, there is little respect forthcoming from this group for organized Christianity, but we would be tragically mistaken if we thought of them as entrenched enemies of the Christian faith. Some might be, but by no means all. When we interviewed the authoress Nell Dunn, she told us that she certainly believed in Jesus Christ, but had little knowledge of God. Her reservations about the Church were even greater. At the time of writing she and her husband, writer Jeremy Sandford, are asking astute public questions and making equally astute public answers on current life and society in such plays and films as 'Cathy Come Home' and 'Poor Cow'. But they are also interested in people's spiritual development. As yet such opinion formers are obviously more aware of the questions than of the answers. If only we can recover the authentic experience, unconquerable faith and meaningful communication that are the hallmarks of original Christianity, we may well earn the privilege of sharing with them the 'answers' which flow from a knowledge of Jesus Christ.

4. GUIDELINES

As we have sought to understand the melting-pot situation in England today and the position of the Church in it, we have been led to certain conclusions which we now summarize under three main headings and offer as guidelines. Our own times seem to be decisive ones in many respects, and it is vital that Christians seize upon the present opportunity with conviction and understanding.

(a) We Must Learn to Listen

The unique authority of the Christian lies in his conviction that through the Bible God does speak to man's needs, but often what we say does not have power in the lives of the people we speak to because we have failed to listen to them first. In fact, the ears are probably the most neglected part of the Body of Christ today. If so, then the implications are both obvious and serious. The man who continually talks loudly, with impregnable self-confidence and without listening, soon finds that conversation becomes a monologue without an audience! Often Christians are so insistent upon repeating again and again the same things in the same way that we almost force people to ignore us. What to us is so important can become a meaningless formula to non-Christians. Whereas nothing can alter the essential nature of Christian truth and the facts of the Gospel which we are

50

to 'press home on all occasions' (2 Tim. 4.2 N.E.B.), it is still quite possible to present the truth in a way that is insensitive to people's personalities or completely lacks an understanding of present-day thinking and culture.

Many Christians today are becoming anxious at their inability to understand what is going on around them – the films, TV plays, pop music, youth cults – and this is a dangerous indication of their increasing isolation and insulation. What we often ignore or turn away from as 'distasteful' or 'irreligious' in modern life only increases our isolation and makes it less possible for non-Christians to understand our message. Somehow our insulation must be broken down. A way must be found through the barrier of self-satisfaction and false confidence which many of us have built around ourselves. Destruction of this barrier may prove painful for some, yet it will free us in new ways to listen with sympathy and understanding to what people are saying. It is hardly good enough to dismiss the Wednesday Play on TV with a snort of disapproval, saying, 'It doesn't mean anything!'. It might well be intended to depict the very meaningless of much modern life. One Christian has astutely called it, 'The Existentialist Religious Broadcast of the Week'. Likewise, is it good enough simply to brand some of today's cults as 'shocking' or 'perverted'? The Christian might well say they are so, but it is all too easy to stop there and erect a barricade instead of seeking to understand the thought background of such movements. Are we simply to condemn the flower children, the hippies, those hooked on drugs – that is, if we ever get close enough to them to speak? There *is* a relativistic way of thinking behind their bohemian living which we would do well to understand if we are to earn the right to talk to them.[34] And even the youngster next

34. Useful analyses of modern thought forms and culture: Francis Schaeffer: *Escape from Reason* (1968, I.V.F.) and *The God Who is There* (1968, Hodder & Stoughton).

door, from a 'respectable' home, seems to be so different in his attitudes and ideas from the youngsters two or three generations back. We can see these attitudes and ideas reflected in the words of many of today's pop songs, art and films. Much modern literature and art says 'man is dead', and many artists, writers and musicians have now accepted and are propagating their belief that the universe is absurd and that there is no unified field of knowledge. Such belief will – or ought to – affect the ways we seek to teach Christian truth. But we must not block our ears to what society is saying, accepting and sharing. If we do, we are in danger not only of losing the hearing of people but also of never regaining it. We need to listen because people will never believe that we care about them until we do. We must listen to *people*, not merely society or culture, and having listened we must never forget that what we have heard is intended to help us speak, clearly, lovingly, and with authority, God's word for man.

Listening will involve some Christians in studies and disciplines which we have tended to neglect in the past. Sociology and psychology are two obvious examples. It will also surely involve some of us in more reading and an informed interest in art forms and culture. Listening will involve every Christian in sympathetic relationships with those around him. In these and other ways perhaps we shall the more effectively become the Body of Christ in England today.

(b) We Must Learn to Communicate

What is it that we want to communicate to non-Christians in England today? We want them to know nothing more nor less than the facts of the Gospel in the context of Christian truth. But possibly one reason why many of us have become depressed about the difficulty of this is that we are confusing Christian truth with traditions, church organizations and

52

structures. Many churches impose standards of conformity upon people which are more a matter of tradition and custom than of true spiritual life. The Rev. Roger Sainsbury underlines this, writing of the youth work at Shrewsbury House, Liverpool: 'Many people I know have been shocked at the way some of our Christians act: they smoke, they drink, they dance to beat music, they don't have regular Quiet Times. "How can they be Christians?" some Evangelicals might even ask. But often their courage in witnessing in most difficult circumstances has put me to shame.' The Rev. David Sheppard writes: 'Ways and speed of Christian growth will vary according to background. We should not look for stereotyped marks of growth in every Christian, whether in the matter, for example, of personal devotional discipline or in what constitutes turning away from worldliness,' [35] – but rather those attitudes described in the Bible as the fruit of the Spirit. At every stage in history there needs to be the readiness to stop and clarify the dividing lines between Christian truth and the traditions, organizations and structures accompanying it which might stand in need of adaptation and change. Whereas God's truth and the teaching of Scripture stands firm and unchanging, we need constantly to demonstrate true flexibility in the methods we use.

What do we want people to see when they look at the Church? The temper of the country's commerce is determined by men who have ruthlessly decided on an image they wish to create and then have given enormous effort to creating that identity in the minds of the consumers. We shall never convince men who live according to those principles that the Gospel is worth their serious consideration until we at least match their determination.

There must be adaptation, but not of the kind which

35. David Sheppard: p. 49, *Mission in the Modern World* (1968 Patmos).

empties the original message of its distinctiveness. Rather we seek the kind of adaptation which enables the message to fulfil its revolutionary rôle in the new environment. The question is not 'How do we make people swallow the message?' but 'How do we present it in a way relevant to their situation?' It *can* be modernized, in the sense that it becomes understandable to the new generation. It *cannot* be modernized in the sense that makes it fit in with the thinking of a new generation. The clue to the solution lies in the Bible itself, for it shows on the one hand how the story of God's dealings with men must be constantly and audaciously told in new ways and new situations. But it shows also very clearly that the central affirmation on which that story is based remains the same, because Jesus Christ is the same 'yesterday, today and forever'. [36]

Without in the least compromising Christian truth and the message of the Gospel, we must show a willingness to distinguish between the content of our faith and the traditional media of communication.

We must also encourage Christians equipped with gifts of communication to think, write, and speak forthrightly. We have too often withdrawn from realms of culture and creativity. The concept of leisure and creativity is important in Christian teaching, yet too often we have made a virtue of contracting out of society and taking refuge in Christian activism. We need Christian writers, dramatists, artists and musicians who will express Christian truth in different ways. If we have not these gifts ourselves, we should give every encouragement to those who can communicate in this way. Evangelicals have in the past often been mistakenly pietistic about the arts, suspicious and afraid of 'worldliness' tainting their message. All true creativity is a gift of God. Its outworking is seen all through the Scriptures, and it is still

36. Hebrews 13:8.

our responsibility as creatures made in God's image to show the validity of the arts in the context of Christian truth.

Another sphere of communication in which we must discriminate and become increasingly astute is in the use of religious language. Amongst philosophers today there is a keen interest in language, especially that used to describe the supernatural. Many Logical Positivists maintain that much religious language is completely meaningless, for it is attempting to describe that which is 'non-sense'. The Christian truth we have to proclaim *is* verbal and rational: we need words to convey it. Yet in these days we need to exercise special care and caution over our use of Christian language and formulae. One journalist we interviewed impressed us deeply when he said that for him the most meaningful Scripture was: 'Now we see through a glass darkly'. By this he meant that for him, and many others, insensitive dogmatism is a real obstacle. 'Preachers either expect me to understand theological belief or to accept what they say.' He was not asking us to offer him that kind of liberalism which says there is no *dogma*; he *was* asking us not to make *dogmatism* an unnecessary hurdle – the distinction here is fundamental. In an age when the whole education system is geared to the encouragement of questioning, we must be prepared to submit to the same discipline. Not only will Christian truth withstand it, but we may fully expect the Holy Spirit to turn this very situation to His advantage.

If the journalist found religious language and dogma a problem, what of the majority of working-class people whose vocabulary and literacy level is far more limited?

An even greater and more subtle danger we face is that many modern people, hearing the language we use, will interpret it in their own thought-forms. Unless we define carefully what we mean they are likely to understand a statement like 'all men are guilty' in terms of psychological guilt only, omitting the vital truth of man's moral guilt before God. If we say that 'Christ can make a difference', they can equally say, 'And so can LSD'. It becomes increasingly necessary for us to understand and carefully define the vocabulary we use in order to ensure that the Christian truth we present is as clear to them as to us. In this respect, Christians need to have more opportunity and training in their churches to become explicit in their faith. The honest questions asked by an increasing number of young people today demand honest answers, not just descriptive personal testimony to a new experience.

But Christian communication is not exclusively a verbal matter. We must also be prepared for our lives to communicate the positive benefits of the Gospel. Purity of life in the individual and in the corporate fellowship of Christians must witness to the truth of our words. In this sense, then, evangelism must affect us all whether we are at church, at work or at home. In our living and speaking it will be our great desire to become mobilized for the extension of God's kingdom.

(c) We Must Regain our Confidence

Finally, we would suggest that there is a confidence that we must regain in our church life today if we are to be the lively, evangelizing fellowships that the New Testament shows in its descriptions of local groups of Christians.

We must regain *a confidence in Christian Truth*. It is hardly sufficient to be able to repeat, as a set formula, the elements of the Gospel. We must not only set ourselves to understand the deep truths of the Gospel we preach but must also get to grips with important Christian doctrines, see their relevance to our contemporary living and be able to explain them to others in a clear, meaningful way. Too often we evade crucial issues and questions that are thrown up as criticisms of Christianity because we have never thought them through for ourselves. Or, again, we fail to relate our beliefs to every part of our living – our work, our recreation, our home-making, our political views – and they become isolated in a watertight compartment instead of being an integral part of our daily living. In this matter churches have a responsibility to mobilize their members in verbal witness and Christian apologetic.

God's truth is fully accessible to examination and testing by any generation and at any stage in history. Because it *is* truth, it is thoroughly consistent and rational and can stand up to any question. This certain fact should cause us to rejoice and be confident. But let us make sure that we do not take refuge in the false confidence of 'isms' or traditions. Our faith must rest in the truth of God as revealed in the Scriptures.

We must each regain *a personal confidence in our relationship to Christ*. Relationship with Jesus Christ lies at the very heart of the Christian Gospel. The Christian, Paul repeatedly told the Colossians, is a person who is 'in Christ', whose life 'is hid with Christ in God' (Col. 2.3). A living, contemporary knowledge of Christ that can authentically meet the challenges of the twentieth century is needed if people are to see Him to be essential in their own living. We must know the daily reality of His living Holy Spirit through whom powers of darkness have and will continue to be put to flight. The victory brought about by Christ's crucifixion and resurrection is absolutely secure. 'In the world you have tribulation', He said to His disciples, 'But be of good cheer, I have overcome the world (John 16.33). If the present scene seems a far cry from victory, we know that total vindication from evil is going to be known and Christ's victory will be understood and clearly seen by all at the appointed time. Christians must affirm Christ's victory in their whole living if the non-Christian world is to understand anything of the positive benefits of our faith.

We must regain *a personal confidence in our position as children of God*. It is sad to see the extent to which Christians today have become depressed, defensive, and introspective. Is it because they have forgotten their position in Christ, or because, despite what they say, they are placarding defeat in their living? There is no place in the Christian for 'confidence in the flesh', that self-aggrandisement which prevents personal conformity to Christ. Yet this does not imply a denial of the personality and gifts that God has given to men and women who, in all their differences, are meant to complement each other in the total unity of the Body of Christ. Paul was able to count his personal assets 'as refuse', yet this did not mean that he emerged as a negative, intimidated, depressed Christian. He was only too aware of the confidence, dignity and authority which his sure standing in Christ had conferred upon him. Christ promises that if we know the truth it will make us free. Perhaps many of us, in new ways, need to become free from ourselves that we might the more effectively be available to serve others and look to their needs. We can, and must, know a new sense of poise, joy and confidence which only the Holy Spirit can give us as we see the need for it and affirm in ourselves and each other that freedom which Christ came to give us.

The melting-pot situation in Britain today is, in some important respects, similar to that in the Graeco-Roman world surrounding Palestine in the days of the Early Church. There was then a widespread questioning of ethical and moral standards, coupled with a blatancy about immoral conduct which is familiar to us today. There were recently developed aids to communication provided by the Roman roads and a common language, matched by the shrinking world of our jet and satellite age. Under the impact of a clear-cut, revolutionary, but personally fulfilling Gospel, some Jews who had been religiously well-grounded responded, strongly undergirded by the insights from their scriptural heritage. But very many Gentiles with no such relevant background or training also responded whole-heartedly out of their great need. There is every reason to suppose that a similar thing could happen in Britain today and that the very insecurity and fluidity of the present social scene could provide the precise situation in which men and women might well turn to Christ on a scale this generation has never seen.

Chapter Two

THE BIBLE SAYS...

5. WHAT IS EVANGELISM?

Definitions of mission, evangelism, witness and service

There are many ways of causing confusion amongst people who ought to be of one mind, but none is quite so effective as using the same word without definition in a number of different senses. The variety of meaning given to such words as 'mission' and 'evangelism' is a source of disturbing confusion amongst Christians. For instance, the word 'mission' sometimes has an all-embracing meaning, and sometimes refers precisely to a series of evangelistic meetings. The word 'evangelism' may indicate either the verbal announcing of the Gospel, or the total impact of Christians upon the non-Christian world. To 'witness' may be to speak to someone about Christ; it may be to live in a way that demonstrates the Gospel.

It is of great importance that these words should be used consistently, and with a clear and recognized meaning, and we must therefore attempt to clarify them. In the New Testament, and in much current usage, the root of the word *mission* is broad and inclusive.[1] It refers to the total activity of God in reconciling individuals to Himself and in transforming society. The word is limited in direction rather than scope, since it is chiefly concerned with those who are unreconciled to God.

1. In the New Testament the noun 'mission' is not used. The New Testament uses the verb 'to send' frequently, but the noun derived from it denotes the person who is sent rather than the activity.

The verb from which we derive the word *evangelism* is used in the New Testament to denote the spoken announcing of the Gospel with a view to the divine regeneration of the hearers. An indication of this is the fact that the word 'euangelion' – good news – is used 76 times in the New Testament, 38 times indicating a specific and recognized content, in phrases like 'God's servant in the Gospel of Christ', and the other 38 times in connection with verbs of speaking or hearing. The word *evangelism* should therefore be restricted in meaning to announcing the message of salvation.

The word *witness* has a double meaning in the New Testament; usually it indicates a verbal declaration of something seen, believed, or experienced. Sometimes, though rarely, it is the quality of life or a particular action which itself constitutes the witness.[2] The emphasis of the New Testament is upon verbal witness, and an action or quality of life is a witness only when its meaning is unmistakably clear. Today the emphasis is sometimes upon words, and sometimes upon life, and this double meaning, though often confusing, serves to emphasize the fact that the only effective verbal witness is the one substantiated by personal experience.

Service also has many different shades of meaning. It includes compassionate action such as famine relief and educational work to meet people's needs. The New Testament use of the word includes preaching, serving man's spiritual needs with the word of God, and worship.[3]

Throughout this report, the word *mission* is used in a

2. The normal use of the word *marturia* may be seen in John 1.7. The use of the same word in 1. Tim. 3.7 is in a derived sense, and is closer in meaning to the word 'testimonial'.
3. *Diakonia*, one of the New Testament words meaning service, is used in Acts 6.4 to describe both preaching the word and 'serving tables'. Another New Testament word for service, *leitourgia*, refers to worship in Acts 13.2 and to compassionate action in Phil. 2.25 and 30: cf. Rom. 12.1.

broad and inclusive sense, denoting the total activity of God in relation to those who are reconciled to Him. *Evangelism* is a limited and precise word, indicating the proclamation of the Gospel, whatever form that proclamation may take. *Witness* is used to refer to a verbal testimony to the transforming power of Christ, a testimony supported by living evidence. *Service* denotes the action Christians take, for the sake of their Master, to meet all aspects of human need.

Clarifying the meaning of these words, important though it is, does not answer a more important question concerning the relation between them, a question which will be considered later.

It is however necessary to expand still further our definition of *evangelism*. The broad use of the word is common today, so common that it can include almost any aspect of Christian activity. In seeking to define the word narrowly and precisely, we are not attempting to deny the significance for evangelism of the fellowship of the Church, or to belittle the interest in the Gospel which an act of Christian service may arouse. We are concerned to emphasize the New Testament truth that evangelism is constituted by the declaration of a specific message in order that the hearers may be converted. Evangelism is not constituted by a particular kind of public meeting, nor by a generous act of service. Evangelism takes place only when a particular message is delivered, and delivered in such a way that, with the help of the Holy Spirit, the hearers may understand both the message itself and its bearing upon their lives. It is obviously necessary therefore to ask what are the essential ingredients in the evangelistic message.

6. THE GOSPEL IN OUTLINE
(a) The Truth about God

The preaching of the Gospel in the New Testament is set within the framework of a knowledge of God. Apart from such knowledge, the truth about man and the Gospel message itself are unintelligible. If therefore the Gospel is to be set down systematically in outline, it is necessary to begin with God, the Creator, Sustainer, and Lord of every aspect of human life and history. His absolute authority, His limitless power, and the glory of His person are the foundation of Christian faith. Clearly, however, the truth about God neither can nor should be separated from the revelation which He has given of Himself in Jesus Christ, as witnessed to by the prophets and apostles in the Scriptures.

God's holiness and righteousness, His love and justice, which He revealed in Old Testament times, are fully displayed in Jesus Christ. Moreover, the New Testament makes it plain that Jesus Christ, who lived in Galilee, was 'in the beginning with God', the agent of creation, and that He has now been given authority and dominion. He is the source of all true life, and the reference point for all knowledge. Truly to preach Christ, in all His glory, is to reveal God, the Creator and Lord, and thus to fill in the background against which the truth about man and the truth about salvation may be understood.

(b) The Truth about Man

The truth about man begins, not with his depravity, but with his dignity. It begins, not with sinners, but with man created in the image of God, and with the one perfect man Jesus Christ. His true humanity and the splendour of His life show us what man ought to be like, made as he is for a life of fellowship with God. Measured by the standard of God's absolute holiness, and compared with the perfection and dignity of Christ, the evil of man's nature becomes glaringly apparent. Every part of his nature is affected by sin, his mind twisted, his affections misplaced and his urge to worship perverted. But it is not enough merely to think of sin as failure or wrong-doing. The Christian faith goes to the root of the matter, and reveals sin as an offence against a holy God, a state of being and a way of life in which God's authority is flouted, His holiness scorned and His righteousness mocked. A genuine conviction of sin is not an uncomfortable feeling that things are not what they might be, nor a desire to turn failure into success; it is based upon a true knowledge of God and a realistic knowledge of man, an awareness of the shattered relationships between them, and a longing that somehow it should all be put right.

(c) The Message of Salvation

At the heart of the Christian message is the death and the resurrection of Christ, two parts of the pivotal event in world history. The presentation of that event must link together carefully the nature of Christ's person and the meaning of his death. Neither must be emphasized to the apparent exclusion of the other; we must proclaim 'Christ-in-His-work', that 'God was in Christ reconciling the world to Himself'.

It is also necessary to emphasize that, in proclaiming the Gospel, the interpretation of the historical events cannot be separated from the events themselves. The fact and its meaning must be indissolubly one, for the significance of Christ's death is not merely that it happened, but that it was a death for sins.

The essence of that significance may be summarized from the New Testament in three propositions:

(a) Sin must be judged. We have seen that all men are caught up in sin, the essence of which is rebellion against God. The very character of God demands that such rebellion be judged. This fact, sombre as it is, nonetheless gives cause for hope, for it demonstrates that God is God, and that man matters to Him.

(b) The judgment on sin is the breaking of the relationship between God and man. The proper dignity and

64

true direction of man's life are derived from his relationship to God. To be separated from Him is therefore to be separated from true life, a fact which is everywhere apparent in our human situation.

(c) The judgment upon sin has been endured for man by Christ. God in Christ has taken the initiative in dealing with our sin and with the judgment upon it. By voluntarily giving himself to die upon the cross Christ suffered the worst that sin can do, including separation from His Father. God laid upon him all the consequences of human wrong-doing and wrong relationships, and He took upon Himself the penalty of our sin. This understanding of the Atonement, which is both clear and prominent in the New Testament, lies at the heart of the various Biblical descriptions of Christ's death – e.g. sacrifice, redemption, justification, reconciliation.[4]

But the cross cannot be proclaimed, and would indeed be meaningless, apart from the resurrection. When God raised Christ from the dead, He broke the power of sin and death, and gave full proof of the fact that Jesus Christ, by His death on the cross, has dealt with sin once for all. By its very nature, therefore, the work of Christ is unique and unrepeatable. What God has achieved does not need to be done again. It is complete, a full atonement for the sins of the whole world.

(d) Repentance and Faith

The fourth part of the Gospel message is a summons to

4. The substitutionary nature of Christ's death has been, and frequently is, travestied as immoral or unjust, and the crudeness of some Evangelical preaching on the Cross has given good grounds for such changes. The importance of our emphasis earlier upon 'Christ-in-His-work' was to make it possible to hold the New Testament paradox, that 'God was in Christ reconciling the world to Himself', and that God 'made Him to be sin who knew no sin, so that in Him we might become the righteousness of God'.

repentance and faith. The two belong together as the two parts of man's response to God's initiative. Repentance is not merely 'feeling sorry', any more than faith is a leap into the unknown. Repentance involves both sorrow for the past, and a genuine change of mind, heart and will. Similarly faith is an act of wholehearted trust in the living God, the God who, in Christ, has shown Himself to be wholly trustworthy. It is commitment to God, based upon knowledge about God.

(e) Forgiveness and New Life

What God promises to those who respond to the Gospel is forgiveness of sins, the gift of the Holy Spirit, a new relationship with Himself, and life in the community of His people. These promises are fulfilled by God as soon as anyone turns to Him, though the transformation of the individual and of his relationships which will result may be either sudden and dramatic or, more usually, gradual.

(f) The Hope of Christ's Return

The preaching of the Gospel recorded in the Acts of the Apostles is frequently carried through to the ultimate event of world history, the personal return of Christ and the final judgment. History is not moving towards any improved society and a world of justice and true humanity. The only progress known in the New Testament is progress towards the final summing up of all things in Jesus Christ. Salvation in the New Testament embraces not only what has happened, and what is now happening, but also what will happen. God is the Sovereign Lord of man and of history, and one day all will be subject to Jesus Christ.

This hope is sometimes explicitly related in the apostolic preaching to the final judgment; Christ is 'The one ordained by God to be judge of the living and the dead' (Acts

10.42). The most fundamental distinction in the judgment is between those who trust Christ and His saving work and those who do not. The former, their lives founded upon Christ, will be accepted as children of God and judged according to the way in which they have built upon that foundation (1 Corinthians 3:10–15). Among the latter, two groups must be distinguished; those who have heard the Gospel presented in such a way that the issues are plain to them, and those who either have never heard of Jesus Christ or have never had the Gospel put to them intelligibly. It is clear from scripture that without Christ, no man is righteous before God. It is equally clear from scripture that those who have heard the Gospel and have chosen to reject it, are by that very choice already condemned to eternal separation from the presence of God.

(g) The Irreducible Minimum of the Gospel

The ingredients of the Gospel as given, though they fall far short of even a full outline, are nonetheless more than is required for saving faith. Yet the attempt to define the irreducible minimum which is essential for saving faith is fraught with danger, for brevity too easily leads to obscurity. It is necessary, however, to summarize that minimum for the sake of later sections of the Report, and at the same time to emphasize that the summary must be understood in the light of the fuller statements already made.

The first essential is belief in Jesus Christ as both fully man and fully God. The second is a realistic understanding of the plight of man as a helpless sinner before a Holy God. The third essential is belief in the atoning death and triumphant resurrection of Christ as the sole means of man's redemption from sin and reconciliation to God. The fourth essential is the response to the work of the Holy Spirit, the response of repentance and faith as a genuine turning from sin and an act of trust in God.

These are the bare essentials of the Gospel; they can neither be reduced nor altered. They do not by any means comprise the whole Christian faith, but without them Christian faith does not exist. The Gospel is described in the New Testament as 'the gospel of God'. It is neither the invention nor the possession of man; it is God's. It is therefore not pride or obstinacy which makes us declare categorically that the essence of the gospel can neither be reduced nor altered. It is a humble recognition of the fact that the gospel is God's, and is therefore true for all men and for all time.

7. EVANGELISM AND THE MISSION OF GOD

The sovereignty of God and the responsibility of man are truths, apparently contradictory, yet placed side by side in scripture. They are to be held with equal emphasis, in the relation in which the Bible sets them; that is, as complementary truths which cannot be reconciled by our finite minds. God's sovereignty is neither limited nor hindered by the responsibility He has given to man, and man's responsibility is neither unreal nor restricted by the fact of God's sovereignty. Our understanding of evangelism must give due emphasis to both truths. So in discussing the work of evangelism, we concentrate first upon the work of God in His sovereignty, and then upon the responsibility of man.

(a) Mission as God's Work

Mission is primarily the work of God. It originates in the nature of God, who is everywhere active in love and in judgment. It is focused in the work of God the Son, through whom alone men are redeemed and reconciled to God. It continues in the work of God the Holy Spirit, who glorifies Christ and gives new life to men.

The primary purpose of God's mission is to make men

new through the Gospel, and through them to bring all aspects of human life into submission to Christ. The focal point of God's mission is therefore the Gospel of Christ, and at the heart of mission lies the work of evangelism.

(b) Spiritual Power in Evangelism

It follows from this that the only true power in mission is the power of God. To engage in mission is to enter into a fierce spiritual conflict between 'the god of this present age' and 'the God and Father of our Lord Jesus Christ'. It is a conflict in which the weapons are those of Divine and not human power.

The events of the Gospel, the death, the burial and the resurrection of Christ, are events in which the extremes of human weakness are displayed. In them, Christ rejected absolutely all forms of human power and secular strength. He relied totally upon the power of God, and the weapons with which He engaged in spiritual conflict were the spiritual weapons of prayer and obedience. The gospel is thus a gospel of Divine power, and reliance upon human wisdom robs the gospel of that power.

Similarly evangelism is essentially a work of God the Holy Spirit. It is His work to glorify Christ, to convict men of sin, and to give repentance and new life. 'The Church's witness will always be subordinate to that of the Spirit. It is less that we do the witnessing and He confirms our testimony, than that He bears the witness and we corroborate His'.[5] The only effective power in evangelism is the power of the Holy Spirit, and reliance upon human strength or technique cramps that power.

(c) Regeneration and Conversion

If the Gospel is the power of God and the only true power in evangelism is the power of the Holy Spirit, we must go on to ask what is God's work in the salvation of the indi-

5. *Our Guilty Silence* : J. R. W. Stott : p. 57.

vidual soul? The words normally used to describe this work are regeneration and conversion, two words which are frequently misunderstood.

By definition, regeneration, or new-birth, is something man cannot do for himself; it is a work of God, and those who are regenerate are described as having been 'born of God'. Similarly by definition, regeneration is an event which occurs at a particular time. The individual may or may not be conscious of it, and a variety of experiences, spread over a long or a short time, may precede it. What matters is not the nature of the experience, but the fact, and a genuine birth 'from above' will inevitably show itself – either suddenly or very gradually – in a transformed life. Therefore on the rare occasions when it is necessary to examine the reality of a person's faith, the question which should be asked is not 'What sort of experiences has this person had?' but 'What evidence is there that this person's life is now being transformed by the Spirit of God?'

The word 'conversion' has acquired rich and wide meaning, and is now used to describe any and every aspect of becoming a Christian. It frequently includes repentance, faith, and regeneration. In Scripture, however, the word has a limited use, and describes the act of human turning. It normally means to turn from one direction into another and is something man does. When therefore it is applied to becoming a Christian, it refers to turning from sin and trusting in Jesus Christ.[6]

6. It has been suggested that in this secular age, conversion should be defined as 'a turning round in order to participate by faith in a new reality which is the true future of the whole creation'. It is 'commitment, in penitence and faith, to what God himself is doing in human history' (All Things New: W.C.C.: p. 43). Such definitions have the advantage of emphasizing that the spiritual life of man is inseparable from and is expressed in life as a whole, and that conversion will affect a man's relationships and experience. But they have the grave disadvantage of ignoring the supernatural aspects of conversion and of obscuring the fact that conversion is primarily turning to Christ, and that everything else flows from the new relationship thus formed.

Regeneration and conversion are thus distinguished from one another, and the distinction is important, particularly in view of the breadth of meaning now attached to the word 'conversion'. But having made the distinction, we must emphasize that the act of conversion is made in response to the initiative and the prompting of the Holy Spirit, and that both repentance and faith are described in the New Testament as the gift of God.

(d) Regeneration and Baptism

It is not possible to be joined to Christ by the Holy Spirit without at the same time being joined to Christ's body, the Church. Being a Christian and being in the Church are the same thing in the New Testament, and both are due to the grace of God. But whereas in the New Testament regeneration and baptism may sometimes have coincided, they are not to be identified. Baptism is not the means of regeneration. In the New Testament, baptism is closely linked to regeneration as the outward sign of God's grace, involving on man's part a responsive commitment to Christ and to His Church. In a sense, therefore, it is true to say that regeneration is complete without baptism, but conversion as defined above is not. Willingness to be fully identified with a local community of God's people is a necessary consequence of regeneration, and an integral part of conversion.

8. EVANGELISM: MAN'S RESPONSIBILITY

In the preceding section, we have sought to lay primary emphasis upon God's sovereignty. Our concern now is to discuss the responsibility which God has entrusted to man in relation to various aspects of evangelism, while at the same time drawing out the practical implications for evangelism of Divine sovereignty.

God's appointed agency in evangelism is the Church.

Though He could have announced the Gospel message in many different ways independent of man, God has in fact chosen to speak through the community of His people. Unless God's people make the Gospel known, the Gospel will not be known. If therefore the Church is to be true to its essential nature, it must be a community which, by the form of its life and the reality of its proclamation, is continually making plain the issues of life and death inherent in the Gospel.

The focal point of God's evangelistic activity is the local church, which is, ideally, the whole company of God's people in a particular locality. It is all the believers in a particular area who are joined in fellowship with Christ and with one another by true preaching of the Word and proper administration of the sacraments.

In practice, however, the local church in almost every place is tragically divided among the denominations, and this is undoubtedly a hindrance to its evangelistic outreach. In addition to this, the community life is often weakened by the increasing mobility of people. Some Christians belong to the church at their place of work, while others will sometimes travel to a church far from their place of work or residence.

It is essential that Christians should belong to a Christian community, and it is important that, so far as possible, they should belong as families. This means in practice that Christians should belong to the local church where they live unless there are strong reasons for not doing so. To travel to another church farther away is to pass a judgment upon the local church, the seriousness of which is not always realized.

(a) Evangelism and the Church

If the local church is to be effective in evangelism, it must be what God intends it to be. First, it must be a worshipping community, a community of people so taken up with God that they are continually praising Him, and being renewed by Him. Second, it must be a genuine fellowship, a community to which people belong and in which they share a variety of experiences God gives them. This means in practice that a congregation of any size must meet not just as one group large enough to maintain corporate fellowship, but also in several groups small enough to make genuine interchange possible. Third, it must be a witnessing community, making an impact upon the world by the holiness of its life and the reality of its proclamation.

There can be no doubt that the vigour and effectiveness of any Church's witness depends very largely upon the quality of its worship and the depth of its fellowship. The fact that there is a renewed interest in worship is therefore cause for encouragement and hope. More hopeful still is the considerable upsurge of interest in the impact of the Holy Spirit upon the total life of the Church. There is a longing, shared today by an increasing number of people, for the full life of the Spirit to be displayed in the Church, and a genuine experience of the fullness of the Spirit always leads to renewed worship, deeper fellowship, and more vigorous evangelism. A full experience of the life of the Spirit is the birthright of every Christian, and the hall-marks of mature spiritual life are renewed worship issuing in greater holiness of life, and deeper fellowship in the Gospel, resulting in more powerful evangelism.

It is in relation to this emphasis upon the Church as the agent of evangelism that the responsibility of individual Christians must be understood. The responsibility for evangelism is laid by God upon the community of His people, and upon individuals as members of that community. The Holy Spirit is a witnessing Spirit; the Church is called to be a witnessing community. Because he is possessed by the Spirit, and a member of the Church, every Christian is bound to share in the work of evangelism. That work is essentially a shared responsibility, in which all will speak for Christ whenever there is an opportunity to do so, all will pray, and some, who are given the particular gift by God, will serve as evangelists.

(b) The Ministry of an Evangelist

Thus it is also within the context of the Church as God's agent in evangelism that the ministry of the evangelist must be understood. It is apparent that Christ gives to certain people the particular qualities required to make the Gospel and its application crystal clear. It is also significant that the word 'evangelist' is used only three times in the New Testament, twice in relation to particular individuals – Philip and Timothy – and once in a passage describing the gifts given by Christ 'to equip God's people for the work of ministry, for building up the body of Christ'.[7] This indicates that the evangelist is not to do the work of evangelism instead of the Church, nor is he to do it apart from the Church. His calling is to serve as a focus for evangelism on behalf of the Church. 'What Christ founded was not an order of preachers, nor the institution of preaching, but a community, a Church, whose first charge His preaching should be. It is Church and preacher together that reach the world'.[8] The evangelist does not receive his gift and ministry from Christ apart from the Church, any more than he receives it from the Church apart from Christ. He receives it from Christ in his Church.

This means in practice that the Church must be ready both to recognize, clearly and publicly, the gift of evangelists, and to make proper provision for their ministry and their support. Correspondingly, it means that the evangelist will serve Christ within the Church, and will, so far as pos-

7. Eph. 2.11.
8. *Positive Preaching and the Modern Mind*: P. T. Forsyth: p. 59.

sible, make the basis of his fellowship a particular local congregation, rather than an independent evangelistic association. This does not of course mean that the evangelist must restrict his ministry to the particular local congregation of which he is a member. The gifts Christ gives are to be used more widely for the benefit of the whole body.

In considering the ministry of an evangelist in relation to the whole Church, it is necessary to make a distinction between churches which are continuously engaged in evangelism and those which are not. The most effective evangelism is carried on through the regular ministry of a church and the unceasing witness of its members, and the more a church engages in this sort of evangelism, the more clearly defined the place of the full-time evangelist is likely to become. Such a church may decide that the ministry of an evangelist is needed for a particular occasion; it may also decide that an invitation to participate in an evangelistic campaign should be refused on the grounds that participation will be a hindrance to the regular and more effective evangelistic work in which the church is engaged. Here is one of the points of stress in the sadly uneasy relationship between evangelists and the churches.

It is likely, however, that there will be greater tension in the relationship between the evangelist and churches which do not engage in evangelistic work. Individual Christians in a certain town, conscious of the failure of the churches to accept their responsibility for evangelism, may seek the help and advice of an evangelist, thereby placing him in a delicate situation. The evangelist ought still to remember that he is to be a focus for evangelism on behalf of the Church, and that his gift is to be used 'for building up the body'. His first concern will therefore be to awaken the churches to their responsibility, a concern which those churches may or may not welcome. If, however, the evangelist is eventually confronted with a clear choice between preaching the Gospel in the face of the persistent failure of the churches, and the Gospel not being preached at all, he must undoubtedly choose the former.

But two further points must be borne in mind in such a situation: first, the evangelist is not only a preacher of the Gospel to the world, but also a prophet to the disobedient churches, and he must be prepared for those churches to treat him with the disdain or opposition customarily reserved for prophets. Second, the evangelist is still a focus for evangelism on behalf of the whole Church, and may expect and should receive the support of local churches in other areas.

(c) 'Follow-Up'

This kind of situation raises in an acute form the question of what is usually described as follow-up. When a church is engaged in regular evangelistic work, this should present few problems. A person is converted both through and into the life of that church. It is when the churches are failing in evangelism, or an individual is converted through the witness of a Christian at work, away from the local church, that difficulties arise.

We have already emphasized that regeneration into the Church is an essential part of the Gospel. If this is to mean anything, it must involve membership of the local Christian community. Follow-up is much more than two Christians meeting together for Bible study and prayer, and the lending of a few helpful books, valuable though this may be. It is the introduction of a new Christian to the total life and fellowship of the church, and this introduction will make heavy demands on the church, in creating, for instance, special opportunities for basic teaching to be given.

In this connection, there are important implications to be drawn from the fact that mission is primarily God's. Because this is so, we should expect that God will lead people to whom He has given new life to find ways of expressing that life which are unusual and perhaps disturbing. We should not expect to find stereotyped patterns of behaviour and an equal speed of growth in all Christians. Too often the fact that mission is God's is forgotten, and the life and development of individual Christians and of the church as a whole is hindered by the eagerness with which new believers are pressed into the patterns of worship and life with which the church is already familiar.

But what is an evangelist to do when the local church is clearly unable or unwilling to, receive new believers? Obviously, he must try to introduce those believers into a fellowship which will receive them. In fact, this question really turns upon what is meant by a church which is 'clearly unable or unwilling to receive new Christians'. We believe that new Christians should be introduced into churches where the Word of God is truly preached, and the Sacraments properly administered, and that an evangelist has a responsibility to exercise care and discernment in this matter. But in practice this does not mean that the evangelist may decide in which churches there is a true ministry of word and sacrament. He must respect the claims of a church to be faithful to God unless those claims prove themselves unfounded, either by a refusal to receive a new Christian or by a failure to give proper teaching and adequate help.

(d) The Relation between Various Aspects of Mission

Our consideration of God's appointed agency in evangelism has led us on to discuss ways and means, and therefore brings us back to a question raised earlier, that of the relation between the various aspects of mission. We have defined mission as the total activity of God in reconciling individuals to Himself and in transforming society. Our emphasis upon the fact that God is Sovereign means in practice that His work in the world is much wider than his work through the Church, and that his mission reaches into all areas of life, including those untouched by the Church. The implications of this for evangelism are important, but it is necessary to emphasize that our definitions have not equated evangelism and mission. Evangelism is an essential part of mission, but mission also includes witness and service.

Evangelism, Identification and Dialogue

The essence of evangelism is the delivery of a message from God; without this there is no evangelism. But the message from God must be delivered in such a way that the hearers understand both the message itself, and its application to their lives. This means that we must grasp the implications of two significant but greatly abused words, 'identification' and 'dialogue'.

The great emphasis today upon identification is to some extent a reaction against false understandings of the biblical teaching about separation from the world. Identification with the world does not mean that the Church must become like the world. It is not the similarity between the Church and the world which attracts people to Christ; it is the difference. Yet belief in God as the Lord of creation and of all aspects of life, and a desire to follow Christ's example, both impel the Christian to be identified with the world. This means a genuine, a full, and a Christian participation in the life of the world. Without such identification, evangelism degenerates into meaningless irrelevance.

Dialogue has become extremely popular in some circles and highly suspect in others. Basically, 'the action of dialogue is one by which a person makes himself available to and aware of others'.[9] The proper contrast is not between dialogue and proclamation but between dialogue and monologue, a contrast in which monologue may be defined as so

9. *The Miracle of Dialogue*: R. L. Howe: p. 75.

great a preoccupation with the message and its delivery that the real situation and needs of the hearers are ignored. Put in these basic terms, the choice between dialogue and monologue is straightforward. Being available to and aware of the other person and seeking to enter deeply and sympathetically into his experience – these are essential if a genuine relationship is to be established. Moreover, the Christian, believing as he does in the sovereignty of God and in the grace of the Holy Spirit, will realize that God is already at work in the experience of the other person, and will treat that experience seriously.

But it is sometimes urged that dialogue can take place only when two people meet on equal terms, as joint seekers after truth, and that the task of the Christian is to reveal the Christ who is already present in the experience of the other person, in order that that experience may be fulfilled. In this sense, the two people do meet on equal terms; the Christian has no grounds for pride or superiority. But the Christian has a message to deliver, a message which is God's truth. He neither can nor should conceal the fact that this message has the authority of God Himself. The Christian will also be aware of the fact that though God is at work, the powers of evil are dominant in the life of the non-Christian, and God's command is that he should repent and believe in the Gospel. We maintain that it is the duty and the privilege of Christians to proclaim this Gospel, and that true proclamation does not inhibit genuine dialogue. Evangelicals have much to learn about dialogue; may we suggest that others may also have something to learn from the evangelical emphasis upon proclamation?

Identification and dialogue are thus of great importance in making the communication of the Gospel possible and meaningful, but we must make one further point in this connection. The Gospel message is God's truth; it is a substantial message about what God has done and can do.

It is therefore a message which cannot be deduced; it must be taught. 'It is by teaching that the Gospel preacher fulfils his ministry. To teach the gospel is his first responsibility: to reduce it to its simplest essentials, to analyse it point by point, to fix its meaning by positive and negative definition, to show how each part of the message links up with the rest – and to go on explaining it until he is quite sure that his hearers have grasped.'[10] We do not of course suggest that there is only one way in which the Gospel can be taught; a great variety of teaching methods should be employed.

Evangelism and Service

It is a sad theological confusion which has led Christians to set evangelism and service against each other, sometimes to the extent of seeing them as mutually exclusive. Some maintain that the sole function of the Church is evangelism, and that service is a worldly distraction; others assert that 'ministry to the secular needs of man in the spirit of Christ is evangelism in the right use of the word.[11] In part this confusion is due, as we have seen, to the different ways in which the words mission and evangelism are used, but definitions do not of themselves clarify the relation between evangelism and service.

Obedient participation in God's mission will undoubtedly involve the Church in both evangelism and service. God is both Creator and Redeemer; His concerns embrace every aspect of human life. The ministry of Christ was a ministry of word and action. And the nature of man, both as an individual and in society, requires a ministry both of evangelism and compassionate service. Full participation in God's mission will involve us in seeking to discern and understand the activity of God in the world. It will involve us in maintaining a clear and unshaken testimony to the

10. *Evangelism and the Sovereignty of God*: J. I. Packer; p. 48.
11. *Rethinking missions.*

80

purposes of God for His world, and to the movement of history towards the summing up of all things in Christ. It will demand costly service, both in meeting the needs of man and in seeking to reform the patterns of society which produce those needs, service which is neither an excuse nor a cloak for evangelism but a genuine expression of the love of God. And it will involve us in meeting the deepest needs of men and women with the Gospel. For the focal point of God's mission, of Christ's ministry, and of man's need, is the Gospel, and evangelism must therefore be the focal point of our obedience in mission.

(e) New Testament Criteria

The final question which we must ask in this section is, what are the New Testament criteria for assessing modern methods in evangelism? First, we must sound a note of warning. It is sometimes suggested that if only we followed the example of the early Christians in evangelism, particularly the example of St. Paul, all our problems would be solved. We certainly should learn from the example of the early Christians, but it is a mistake to treat the patterns of evangelism in the New Testament as exclusive precepts. The situation which St. Paul faced was in some vital respects quite different from that which confronts many Christians today. He could speak in the same language to a great variety of people. He could work in strategic centres and know that the Gospel would be carried from them along the main trade routes. And most important of all, there was in every city a nucleus of people whose background of thought and life was ideally suited to the reception of the Gospel. This helps to account for the fact that in less than ten years the Church was established in four provinces of the Roman Empire through the work of St. Paul. Today, it is frequently necessary to work for up to ten years before the nucleus of a church is established in a single locality, and this is not necessarily because the Gospel is presented with less power, but because the evangelist has to start much further back. In such a situation, the methods used may be vastly different from those of St. Paul; the fundamental principles must be the same.

There is one basic principle which must be observed and applied to all forms of evangelistic activity. We have emphasized that the essence of evangelism is the declaration of the Gospel with a view to the divine regeneration of the hearers. The vital principle is, therefore, Will this evangelistic activity serve the Gospel of God? From this basic question a number of others stem. For instance, will it be a means of making the Gospel and its application as clear as possible? Will it convey the nature of the Gospel as a message from God, with His authority, or will it give the impression that the Gospel can be treated lightly?

The question of whether evangelism is true or not must also be decided by this principle, and not by the results produced. God is Sovereign in evangelism; *He* saves, and not man. The results of evangelism are therefore in His control, and the test which an evangelist must apply to his ministry is not 'How many converts were there?' but 'Was the Gospel made so clear and did it appear so relevant that the hearers understood its application to their lives?' The answer to that question should be apparent through honest questioning in the light of the Scriptures and personal conversation with those who listened. These are some of the questions which may be derived from an honest and a searching application of the cardinal principles.

Other principles, sometimes with a more limited application, may be derived from the aspects of the theology of evangelism already outlined. For example, the Church is God's appointed agency in evangelism. One must therefore ask, 'Does a particular activity serve to extend, to focus or to stimulate the evangelistic work of the local church, or does it in any way hinder that work?' If it is clearly a hindrance, or on balance more of a hindrance than a help, then that activity ought not to be pursued, however good it may be in itself.

In summary, the cardinal principle is that true evangelism serves the truth of the Gospel as fully as possible, and other criteria may be established by drawing out the practical applications of the biblical theology of evangelism.

9. CO-OPERATION IN EVANGELISM

We have already made the point that the responsibility for evangelism is laid by God upon the whole community of His people, and upon individuals by virtue of their membership of that community. Evangelism is therefore essentially a community venture, a co-operative enterprise in which every member of the community is called to play a full part. Fellowship in the Gospel involves fellowship in making the Gospel known.

In the complexities of today's situation, the question of co-operation in evangelism is a difficult one, and because it bears upon the essence of the Christian Gospel, it is a subject which arouses deep feelings. It is therefore a subject which requires careful treatment.

First, we must re-emphasize that the basic principle by which all evangelistic activity must be tested is that true evangelism serves the truth of the Gospel as fully as possible. This principle must be applied rigorously and honestly to the practical issues of co-operation in evangelism.

Next, it is necessary to make some distinctions between people with whom the question of co-operation arises. These distinctions are not made in order to categorize people, nor do we suggest that people can be neatly fitted into one or other of these compartments. They are made for the sake of clarity in discussion.

In order to make these distinctions clear, we must repeat

83

the summary of the essentials of Christian faith given in Section 2, with a reminder that the summary must be understood in the light of the fuller statements made in Sections 2 and 3. The first essential is a belief in Jesus Christ as both fully man and fully God. The second is a realistic understanding of the plight of man as a helpless sinner before a Holy God. The third essential is belief in the atoning death and triumphant resurrection of Christ as the sole means of man's redemption from sin and reconciliation to God. The fourth essential is the response of repentance and faith as a genuine turning from sin and an act of trust in God.

In the last analysis, there is only one distinction to be made; that is, between those who believe in the essentials of the Gospel and those who do not. This fundamental distinction is drawn sharply in the New Testament, as sharply as the difference between darkness and light, death and life.

There are, however, differences both of substance and of emphasis between those who believe in the essentials of the Gospel, just as there are differences between those who do not, and it is necessary to make some of those differences clear.

First, there are those who believe in the essentials of the Gospel, and who derive those essentials from the supreme authority, full inspiration and entire trustworthiness of the Scriptures. Such people believe that this attitude to Scripture is essential if the truth of the Gospel is to be preserved in the Church, and also that Christian life and experience will be seriously impaired without it. But they do not believe that this attitude to Scripture is an essential of the Gospel.

There are others who share the same beliefs in the essentials of the Gospel and the same attitude to the Scriptures. But they maintain that belief in the essentials of the Gospel cannot be separated from belief in the full inspiration and supreme authority of the Scriptures, and they therefore assert that such belief is both essential to and an essential of the Gospel.

The third group consists of those who believe in the essentials of the Gospel, and, though not accepting the attitude to Scripture of the two groups already mentioned, neither add to nor subtract from those essentials in evangelism.

Among those who do in fact believe in the essentials of the Gospel, there are those who add some aspect of the Church's teaching to the essentials of the Gospel, and in doing so, falsify the message.

Others falsify the Gospel by subtracting from it. They believe in the historic facts of Christ's death and resurrection, but maintain that those facts must be preached without any interpretation. Their concern is that the events of the Gospel should speak for themselves as the supreme example of the love and the power of God, and they do not accept the biblical interpretation of the meaning of Christ's death as an essential part of the Gospel.

Others also falsify the Gospel by subtracting from it, but in a different way. They believe, rightly, that the Gospel must be translated into modern idiom. But instead of producing a theology for the secular world, they produce a secularized theology, devoid of any supernatural elements and sometimes detached from its historic basis as well. The result is no Gospel at all, and therefore a natural and sometimes exclusive emphasis upon Christian service.

We believe, as a general guide, that the first three groups ought to co-operate in evangelism among themselves, but that co-operation with the last three groups is impossible. In practice, however, it is more complex than that, and the practical implications of this general guide must be worked out in relation to particular situations.

In the local situation, the question of co-operation usually arises when a united campaign is suggested and various churches are invited to participate. Denominational problems obviously arise in this situation, but if the essentials of the Gospel will be faithfully preached, and if participation in the campaign will not be more of a hindrance than a help to the regular evangelism in which the churches ought to be engaged, then there should be full and energetic co-operation.

Where, as sometimes happens, there is a mixed team of speakers, and the Gospel is to be preached in one meeting but not in the next, the decision is very difficult. Evangelicals ought to be in a position to prevent this situation from arising, but if it cannot be avoided, full co-operation in the campaign would be impossible.

Looking at the problem from the other end, when evangelists are invited to churches where the essentials of the Gospel are not normally preached, we believe that the invitation should be accepted provided that the preaching of the Gospel will not be compromised in any way. Even when they are invited to preach on two nights out of six, and on the other four the Gospel will not be preached, it is surely better that the Gospel should be preached twice than not at all, though this situation could hardly be described as co-operation in evangelism.

Occasionally, a person who believes in the essentials of the Gospel is invited to speak at the same meeting as someone who does not. Obviously there can be no co-operation between them, but there can and should be debate, or dialogue, and both the publicity and the form of the meeting should make clear what is happening.

Co-operation of the sort we are advocating clearly involves risks. But the Gospel is God's power unto salvation. It does not need to be guarded protectively or hedged about with human safeguards. The surest defence of the Gospel is vigorous proclamation of it, in every place and in every situation where that proclamation will be unhindered. A refusal to preach the Gospel is only justified when the opportunity does not in fact exist – that is, when the circumstances of a meeting or the terms of an association make uncompromised proclamation impossible.

10. MOTIVES FOR EVANGELISM

So far we have been concerned with the origins, the content and the proclamation of the Gospel. Our final concern is with the motives for evangelism. Though there are a great many motives for evangelism, there are three primary ones which arise out of the theology of evangelism already outlined. The first is a concern for God's glory; the second, the constraint of Jesus's love; and the third, the inward compulsion of the Holy Spirit.

The Christian is granted the supreme privilege of 'seeing the light of the knowledge of the glory of God in the face of Christ'. He knows that God is the Creator and Lord of all life, a God of power and great glory. He knows from Scripture and experience that God reveals Himself as a God of love in a personal and intimate way, and in doing so, meets man's deepest needs. The Christian ought therefore to be deeply grieved when men dishonour God, and he will be under a compelling and urgent desire to preach the Gospel in which God's glory, His power and His love are fully displayed.

Similarly, the Christian knows that he has been 'ransomed, not with perishable things such as silver or gold, but with the precious blood of Christ'. The wonder of the love of Christ in dying on the cross ought never to grow dim, and that love will arouse in the Christian an ever-growing sense of gratitude. This gratitude will lead first to a desire to do all Christ's will, including His command to 'go and make disciples'. The strongest evangelistic incentive is not the command itself, but sheer gratitude to Christ, and the expression of that gratitude will gain its direction from the command. Secondly, gratitude produces a desire to share the Gospel. Recognizing that all he is and all he has are due entirely to the sheer grace of Christ, the Christian, and only the Christian, can look realistically at the human situation. With no grounds for pride, and no reason for any sense of superiority, he can face up to the appalling needs and sufferings of men as they really are. And knowing what man is, and what Christ can do about it, he will again be under an urgent and compelling desire to preach the Gospel of the transforming love of Christ.

The third motive is the inward compulsion of the Spirit. It is the work of the Holy Spirit to glorify and bear witness to Christ. The promise given to the Apostles, 'You shall receive power when the Holy Spirit has come upon you' was followed, not by a command, but by a statement: 'And you shall be my witnesses'. The gift of the witnessing Spirit leads to witnessing Christians. The Christian, having received the Holy Spirit, ought always to be 'filled with the Spirit' and he will find himself under an inward compulsion to preach the Gospel of new life in the Spirit.

Thus the deepest and strongest incentives to evangelism arise out of the heart of Christian theology, and true evangelism is a natural expression of full and genuine Christian experience. Christians will not engage in evangelism because they are subjected to unceasing exhortations to do so. Evangelistic incentives are zeal for God's glory, the constraint of the love of Christ, and the inward compulsion of the Holy Spirit. If Christians are to take their full share in the responsibility for evangelism which God has laid upon the community of His people, there must first be a deep renewal of true spiritual life, and second, there must be clear teaching about the evangelistic activity in which that life is to be expressed.

Chapter Three

AMBASSADORS ANONYMOUS

The Report of the Practical Group

Any Commission on Evangelism should try to set out what is being done, although any such attempt must produce an inadequate result.

Evangelism means a gang of teenagers patching up the rotten floor of a disused pub in Loughborough, so that it can be opened as a Coffee Bar. Evangelism is a group sitting round a polished desk in the wall-to-wall carpeted offices of an Evangelistic Association discussing a West End première for a film. And it is the pastor of a back-street chapel chatting to a stranger in a hospital ward. We may define it in theological terms; we cannot begin to summarize its practical outworking.

What follows, then, is an admittedly partial look at some areas of evangelistic effort in England today. Many will read this and protest that *their* particular interest or activity has been omitted or misrepresented – we can only plead limited resources of time and money along with the tremendous complexity of the work being done. We recognize that such statistics as we have been able to obtain are limited, and we have tried to avoid drawing unwarranted conclusions or using them to support preconceived ideas.

It must also be emphasized that since this Commission was set up by the Evangelical Alliance, most of the information here comes from sources within the 'evangelical' world; much else is going on, of course, and omissions are not intended to be a judgment on other activities.

11. CHURCHES AND RELATED INSTITUTIONS

(a) Churches

A number of churches in different parts of England were the object of enquiry by means of a structured interview process. They were visited by members of the Commission who used an agreed questionnaire for this purpose.

The Survey covered five Baptist, three Pentecostal, one Congregational, three Independent Evangelical, six Anglican and two Methodist Churches, two Christian Brethren assemblies, and one Salvation Army Corps. Apart from the run-of-the-mill situations, two of the churches are city-centre, three are rural, two are in new towns, three are in new housing development areas, one is in a depressed area, and two are more generally 'downtown'. The churches are scattered over the country.

Few of these churches were chosen for their 'renown'. Not one of the churches registers decline during the past ten years. Some simply maintained their membership level and others multiplied.

This enquiry raises very sharply the whole question of what we mean by 'success'. Most think of success in terms of numerical strength, like the city-centre church that 'trebled in 20 years'. Inevitably, as numbers increase, giving increases, more candidates for the ministry come forward, and the amount of activity accelerates; but numbers are deceptive. A church with a comparatively large congregation – say, an attendance of 500 – may be drawing from a catchment area of 100,000 people. Attendances at village churches are low but they are set among few people. A big old building with a reasonable congregation tends to depress; the same congregation in a small building will elate.

A church, small in numbers, set in a mining village, is described as 'the most successful village church I've ever seen'.

If success is geared to 'output' there is no easy way of assessing it. One well-known city-centre preaching type of church with a congregation of 500 to 700 has a large income, but it works out at 2/6d. per head per week, compared with a little-known gospel hall where the average is 12/– per head per week.

Is success to be thought of in terms of goodwill? One village church is held in good esteem, whilst another village church, with an equal record of comparative success, has suffered persecution.

Is success to be thought of in terms of maturity? A numerically strong church was described by some as 'frothy', whereas a numerically static church gives every indication of being well-taught, well-informed.

Is success to be thought of in terms of men and women exported for the ordained ministry? A congregation of 100 can produce two couples in five years – a much bigger congregation may see no one sent out.

Is success somehow related to doctrine? Every church concerned claimed to give a balanced diet of teaching.

The importance of leadership is apparent. Growth is attributed to 'the vitality and vision of the minister'. Leadership in most churches of every denomination is thought of in terms of 'the minister'. The churches that function without a paid ministry show least signs of growth. (See separate report on the Christian Brethren, which follows.) 'No big increase over 20 years,' says one of them. Some churches clearly recognize that leadership involves both ordained and lay. 'Right leadership essential in every department'. One Anglican church without outstanding leadership has seen remarkable growth by the sharing of responsibility.

'Most of these churches would agree that there are 'no new *methods* of evangelism'. The common emphasis is on 'personal outreach'. 'Friendship is important.' 'Evangelism done on purely social basis between friends and not through street evangelism.' Visitors to an effective Baptist church report 'refreshing lack of gimmick'. Time after time the emphasis is on personal friendliness. 'We have always depended on personal contacts rather than organized outreach – no special stunts.' 'A continuous policy of outreach pervades all policies and departments.'

The importance of the *personal touch* has helped to foster the use of house meetings in contrast to district crusades, literature, and open-air evangelism. There is very little organized involvement by churches in the social structure of the community. The churches' social interest usually is limited to 'giving local old-age pensioners treats and film shows'. The city-centred Salvation Army work amongst drug addicts and social misfits is the exception.

Most of these churches are prayer-related. Weekly prayer meetings on the whole are not well attended, though one with a congregation of 180 records a prayer-meeting attendance of 50 to 80. Another with a congregation of 450 has a prayer-meeting attendance of 150. Most of the churches depend upon the prayers of individuals rather than organized prayer.

Team work is important for effective outreach. 'Reasonable and outspoken unity on the staff team', makes an impact. Unity and agreement between Christians certainly attract. 'Team work of members is wonderful.' The Methodist system of frequent change of ministers brings its problems. One such church run largely by its members has to keep 'a close eye on . . . the ministry'!

Evangelistic crusades, on the whole, come in for criticism. Converts from crusades are mentioned in many of these churches. The Billy Graham Crusades initially attracted, but there are signs of increasing disillusionment. One church had 100 enquirers in 1961; in 1966 they ran trains to the Crusade, but in 1967 they ran 'one train only'. Church-centred crusades fare little better. 'Two held but not enthusiastic – discouraged, in fact.' 'Our October Crusade disappointing – number gained was practically cancelled out by losses – *i.e.*, those who did not care for methods of visiting evangelist.' Nevertheless, it remains true to say that many of these churches owe their very existence to an evangelistic effort or to a crusade of former days.

In recent years there has been an increasing emphasis on *the family*. 'Growth since introducing family worship.' The trend is away from children's work detached from adult worship.

A great deal of *visiting* is done by the churches. Visiting campaigns, house-to-house visiting, sick visiting, membership roll visiting, are described. The emphasis in nearly every case is, however, on the word 'Come'. 'The Gospel is spread by drawing and attracting rather than by going out and bringing them in' is the opinion of more than one. 'Going out to win them' is usually interpreted as going out to get them to come to an evening service where the Gospel is preached. Evangelism is church-building centred. An exception is to be found in a parish church working on a new estate – population 6,500 – where so few attended the evening service that worship is now conducted in houses. Even there the evangelistic guest service is conducted in the building of the church.

It is questionable whether any of these churches touch the working classes. One city-centred Pentecostal church laments, 'Not touching working classes, only professional types.' But the same is reflected in reports on churches working in Local Authority housing estates.

Very practical problems of siting and architecture affect impact. The uninviting building gives the wrong impression.

93

New life came to a church that demolished a Victorian central hall and replaced it by a modern church. The area is downtown and depressed, 'the image completely changed with the new church'.

The only item of *literature* used extensively is the tabloid *Challenge*. One village church says, 'The greatest impact made has been through the distribution of *Challenge*.' It is used in every kind of church. Some churches regularly distribute it house-to-house; others make a special effort with it from time to time. Ready-made booklets frequently mentioned are *Journey into Life*, *The Way Ahead* (CPAS), the Victory Tracts, the John Stott booklets (IVF), Scripture Gift Mission literature and the *War Cry*. Bookstalls are prominent. One or two bookstalls are 'thriving'.

Training in evangelism is a missing factor. Usually the only training is associated with membership instruction. One well-staffed city centre church has a regular training school scheme. One Anglican church in a residential area has worked to release the vicar so that he can run courses in the 'art of personal evangelism'.

There is little or no organized strategy for the *follow-up* of the newly-converted. There is the odd reference to a 'beginners' class', but usually it is restricted to the supply of an enquirer's booklet like *Becoming a Christian*. *Basic Christianity* (also by J. R. W. Stott) is also used. Immediate counselling of enquirers at a guest service is usually regarded as adequate. The process of integration is left very much to the initiative of individuals.

Preaching is the dominant evangelistic weapon of many churches. This is particularly true where a church draws from a very wide area – the emphasis very much on preaching. Preaching is associated with teaching, and evangelism follows. Powerful preaching produces a congregation which thinks of evangelism in terms of bringing the outsider to hear the preacher. 'Key method of evangelism is personal introduction by a Christian to services for special occasions.' 'We rely on the activity of members to bring friends to the services.'

Christian Brethren

Just as the final draft of this Report was being prepared, we received a copy of a very recent survey of evangelism prepared for the Christian Brethren Research Fellowship, and we are grateful for permission to make use of its contents. It relates to Christians who do not normally feature in denominational and similar returns.

The survey was undertaken in the summer of 1966 amongst assembly elders and youth leaders. In most cases the interview was conducted by volunteers. The objects of the study were primarily to discover the place of evangelism in the Church's aims, its evangelistic endeavours, their results and areas of success or otherwise. Seventy-five assemblies in England and Wales were contacted. It was not by any means a random sample, but every effort was made to cover all sizes and types of 'Open' assembly in each part of England and Wales, rural as well as urban.

About two-fifths of assemblies contacted had less than 40 adult members and the same proportion more than 60. The most common group was between 20–39 in size; less than one-fifth of the assemblies contacted had more than twenty children attached to them.

Only one-third of the leaders thought that there had been a decline in membership, while one-eighth had seen a dramatic increase. In only half of these latter cases was it a large increase in membership resulting from conversions.

All assemblies included evangelism in their aims and nearly half quoted it as being their church's primary aim. The remaining assemblies were divided between those who chose the aim of corporate worship and the rest who saw their church's main task in terms of fellowship or exemplifying the New Testament pattern of church gathering. Secondary aims included evangelism amongst young people and a teaching ministry designed to build up Christians.

Practically every assembly had a weekly service primarily to proclaim the Gospel, while nearly all had a Sunday school.

About half had activities which were aimed at young people belonging to the Church, while the same proportion had regular meetings aimed at women.

Just over a quarter had a midweek activity they called a Youth Club but few of these clubs had as extensive a range of activities as most secular youth clubs.

Just over a quarter had a Covenanter group – an activity which is for boys (and sometimes girls) in the lower teens. This seems to be a method used by many assemblies to attract those youngsters who consider themselves too old for Sunday School and to whom membership of a group has big attractions.

About a quarter of assemblies had a Young Wives' group – usually aimed at (as its name suggests) a younger age group than the normal women's meeting and often held in the evening rather than the afternoon.

Nearly all assemblies had a weekly 'Gospel meeting', the chief aim of which was to convey an evangelistic message to non-members.

Although the most popular evangelistic effort, the gospel meeting is also the most criticized; when asked to comment on the ineffective areas of their evangelism, the Gospel meeting was suggested by over a quarter of assemblies. Criticisms ranged over form, timing, concept, and the inability to reach effectively those for whom it is designed.

Six of the assemblies contacted had Family Services on Sunday morning, but there was no evidence that these were any more effective at reaching outsiders. Two-thirds of the churches questioned used door-to-door visitation to advertise their Gospel service, but it is clear to many that this might well be a more effective medium of evangelism in its own right than the Gospel service. Most rely on personal visitation or their notice board to attract visitors.

The table following compares the numbers of conversions claimed by each church in the last two years with the numbers undergoing baptism in the same period.

Numbers of Conversions or Baptisms in the last 2 years	Baptisms Nos. of Churches		Conversions Nos. of Churches	
		%		%
0– 4	44	58	41	54
5– 9	15	21	14	19
10–19	10	13	5	7
20+	3	4	5	7
Don't know	3	4	10	13
	75	100	75	100

Only one thing is common to those churches which recorded ten or more conversions – that is, *an enthusiastic concern on the part of a group or even one person within the church for the task of evangelism.*

Our only further comment would be that we must agree with those who sponsored the inquiry – 'the fact that the information has been vouchsafed at all would indicate that all the assemblies are at the "open" end of the spectrum'; this suggests that it comes from those assemblies most likely to have an active evangelistic concern.

Efforts have been made to reach coloured people and other immigrants. One church says that they have 'no special efforts, to avoid colour emphasis.' Another church has special evenings for specific nationalities. There are difficulties experienced: 'racial discrimination is by no means one-sided; it is difficult to persuade these families really to mix in the church.' In another area where there are many coloured people there are only a few in church – reasons given for not being there are 'forms of worship, reluctance to be committed and to take responsibility.' One church sees no need for action on this point because 'there are several churches in the neighbourhood for coloured people.'

(b) Colleges

All the evidence suggests that ministers have a key rôle in the life of churches today. Whatever we may say as to the desirability of this, it means that those responsible for their training must accept considerable responsibility for the evangelistic effectiveness of the churches. Because of this we sent a questionnaire to 33 evangelical theological and Bible Colleges, 29 of which replied.

What follows is a summary of the outstanding points drawn from this information, seen in the light of the evangelistic task today.

There appears to be an inadequate amount of attention given in colleges to those areas of psychological and sociological study which will equip ministers to interpret behaviour and understand human needs. Similarly, we observe a serious lack of attention to the understanding and use of mass media; this is particularly serious in view of the development of local broadcasting, with the added opportunities that this is giving to ministers. The cultivation of a critical faculty in relation to television and cinema can help a minister to interpret the mood of the times in which he works.

A good deal of attention is given to preaching, but the question arises as to whether those who give instruction are able to assess the evangelistic effectiveness of what the students are saying. Professional theologians and academics are a long way removed from those cultural areas of greatest need. Practical work in evangelism is quite prominent in college programmes, particularly in vacation time. There are signs of growing interest in evangelism as a subject, with diplomas, lecturers, and advanced courses beginning to appear.

(c) Denominations

This section does not attempt to deal with all the evangelism carried on by all the churches in a given denomination. It relates only to information coming from central bodies, dealing with combined efforts of one kind and another in the general area of evangelism.

The following is the result of research carried out on fourteen 'denominations'. They were all asked for their Year Book, but some were only able to supply a letter as they do not publish a book.

Assemblies of God	General Conference Report.
Methodist London Miss. Dept.	London Community and London Mission '67 Report.
F.I.E.C.	Letter (No report issued).
Salvation Army	Annual Report.
Elim Pentecostal	Letter (No report issued).
Presbyterian Church	Extract from report of General Assembly.
Baptist Home Mission	Annual Report.
Free Church of England	Convocation Report.
Strict Baptists	Annual Report.
Independent Methodists	Annual Meeting Handbook.
Wesleyan Reform Union	Year Book.
Congregational Church	Council Report.

Church of England	Year Book.
Methodist Home Mission	Annual Report.

It is difficult to give an accurate report on each denomination's stated evangelistic work as some handbooks rather neglect this subject. Finance tends to loom large. Some letters indicate that they regard evangelism as the work of the local church. Because of these reasons it may appear that the results are unbalanced, but on the other hand this could give an indication of how important a subject it is to these denominations – i.e., the place it finds in the Year Book.

Nearly all denominations have a Mission or Evangelism Committee that sponsors projects and campaigns, and calls to prayer. Nearly all of them mention the Billy Graham Crusades as being valuable. Few seem to be suggesting an overall plan or programme of evangelism through the local church, but most leave the matter to individual churches.

Assemblies of God

They intended using radio widely, although broadcasting on Radio Caroline had to be halved because of finance. They were still short of the £10,000 target set in 1961 for Homeland Evangelism.

They run a scheme for loaning tape recordings which can be used for evangelism. Fourteen major crusades were held in 1967 and seven of them were pioneer efforts. Twelve new Assemblies were added but eleven deleted.

Methodist London Mission Dept.

Evangelism gets a brief mention at the end of the president's report. Christian drama is being used, but on a somewhat limited scale. Work among immigrants is being carried on, especially in areas like Brixton and Bayswater.

F.I.E.C.

No report issued. A missionary approach is being made in Northumberland, Dorset, and mid-Wales; the evangelistic workers, with their caravans, are being supported from outside the areas concerned. Emphasis is on local church responsibility.

Salvation Army

The Joy Strings Gospel beat group have greatly helped by their use of radio, TV, records and rallies, but they have now disbanded. There are, however, about 200 other such groups in the Army.

Open-air meetings are conducted by all of the 1,228 Corps, Societies, and outposts. Social work itself brings its rewards, and it is claimed that 500 men came to the penitent form during 1967 through such work.

Six new evangelistic centres have been opened and fifteen places extended.

Elim Pentecostal

Evangelism falls into two main classes: Movement-sponsored evangelism through the efforts of the Evangelism Committee; and local church-sponsored evangelism.

The committee encourage crusades in towns where there is no Elim Church, with a view to opening one. They state: 'We continue to face the twin problems of availability of halls suitable for crusades and follow-up. Investigations have been made . . . but a great deal of work has produced disappointing results.' There were only two 'pioneer crusades' in 1967 and four other crusades in towns where Elim churches already existed.

A youth committee is responsible for evangelism through special projects such as youth camps. Local churches usually engage in outreach themselves. This includes door-to-door visitation, personal work, coffee bar work and Gospel services.

Presbyterian Church

The emphasis here is that evangelism is the responsibility of the local church and is left to them. Their report therefore gives little help in the matter. They do assert that 'Evangelism is the golden thread that runs through Christian Education, Christian Stewardship, and the Ministry of Healing', and that the training of lay workers is vital to evangelism.

Baptist Home Mission

The Home Work Fund makes possible evangelism in new areas. Ministers are receiving training at the Churches Television Training Centre and a new study outline is being used to train laymen in the responsibility of mass media. Ministers and students are also encouraged to train at courses on Industry and Evangelism. Summer Schools and Camps are held. Over 400 young people attend each year, and the programmes include evangelism. Many youth weekends are also held with this in view. Evangelistic work among immigrants is carried on; a Baptist Jamaican minister is working in the Brixton area.

'Time for God' is a new scheme for young people between 16–30 who serve as volunteers for not less than one month. Included in the choice of jobs is 'evangelism'. 'One Step Forward' Campaigns (pioneered by the Rev. Bryan Gilbert, a member of our Commission) with an inner mission and evangelistic thrust, have caught on, and brought many to the Faith and to church membership.

Free Church of England

In one Diocese more than fifty per cent of the reports mentioned evangelism of some kind; but the Northern Diocese had only one reference, and that was to support for the Billy Graham Crusade.

Strict Baptists

The Report gave no information on our subject; independent church groups are, by definition, bound to put the onus for evangelism on the local churches.

Independent Methodists

The President urged the need for Evangelism in the churches on the 'Crusade Team' lines. 'Decisions' recorded at local churches campaigns were low. Film units are being used effectively. There has been some interest in the possibility of appointing an Evangelist. Youth week-ends have proved successful. An 'Evangelistic Campaign' to cover all the churches was launched in 1967 to last for two years. This is one of the very few total programmes launched by any denomination. An appreciation of evangelism is growing throughout this denomination.

Wesleyan Reform Union

They are running a 'One Year Campaign' aimed at deepening spiritual life and producing better Christian workers. Conferences and a week for young people were conducted.

Congregational Church

The Report says that Home Mission is the business of the County Unions and local churches. The training of lay members is vital to evangelism. Industrial Evangelism is taught to ministers.

Church of England

It has been said that the genius of the Church of England is the parochial system. Evangelism is very much the work of the local clergy, who are to be found in parishes of similar extent but with varying populations. Many feel that this system is outdated and more suited to the England of previous centuries, but others are glad of the systematic representation of full-time workers over the country. Should the Paul and Fenton Morley reports be implemented, this may well affect evangelism.

Since the publication of the report *Towards the Conversion of England* by an Anglican Commission after the 1939–45 War, an advisory board has been in existence to aid Diocesan evangelistic ventures such as the recent mission to Blackburn.

A renewed concern has come for evangelism in the setting up in July 1967 of a new Council on Evangelism (Chairman, the Bishop of Coventry) which is considering 'the mission of the church with special reference to evangelism in its broadest aspects within the contemporary situation. It will endeavour to encourage local churches in their task of mission and will gather and disseminate information about activities which are helping to make more effective the Church's presentation of the Gospel today.'

Methodist Home Mission Report, 1966–7

Creative Groups: 'There is an almost nuclear explosive power in a dedicated group.' 'Shy reserved people are released from inhibitions. Fresh ideas, new unities, new compassions . . .' In a group the walls of partition go down; it represents the most important single recovery of early church practice.

Evangelism is a specialized part of total mission. Both are needed and mutually dependent. Mission must be permanent and not spasmodic, though there is a place for special brief campaigns. 'Mission means the reconciling of God and man and *man and man*'. Billy Graham campaigns show the possibility of co-operation; this must not be lost. 'Are we ready to leave comfortable familiar ways for costly and disturbing mission? There is almost a complete failure of the Church to meet and understand the working man.'

Mission is not a clerical monopoly – it is the task of every member.

Genuine caring for others is important. At one Birmingham meeting of a church which 'goes out' as well as 'brings in', there were converted a civil servant, a cellar beatnik, a student, and a Malaysian Buddhist.

Reference to the work of Cliff College, traditionally a nurture-point of evangelism in Methodism, emphasizes the importance of coffee bar evangelism.

12. SOCIAL AND RELATED GROUPS
(a) Schools

Direct evangelism by teachers is not professionally acceptable, but many young people, particularly those of secondary school age, have been assisted in their faith through Religious Education in schools. The previous position of apathy over R.E. in schools has changed remarkably in recent years. It is interesting to note the current Inter-Varsity Fellowship policy to strengthen the hand of the Christian Education Fellowship; the planned personal membership of teachers associated with the Inter-School Christian Fellowship; and the inception of a new association for Christian R.E. teachers. There is a special need for Christian teachers who take subjects other than R.E., and who will be involved with boys and girls in every area of knowledge. All this *is* relevant to direct evangelism of young people in the school setting outside of lessons and in wider spheres, for a great deal of mass evangelism presupposes a knowledge of the Law and the Gospel. If humanist objectors won the day, the whole approach to evangelism in the country could be affected and might need drastic alteration. Some youth workers told us they would prefer completely secular education with ignorance of the Gospel rather than the confusion of thought now prevailing.

Against this background it is interesting to assess the

work of agencies with access to schools. Professional evangelists are increasingly making a bid to conduct school assemblies and take lessons within the R.E. timetable and extra-curricular gatherings, usually within the framework of an area, city or church campaign.

The Inter-School Christian Fellowship has had remarkable growth in the twenty years since its founding, with 800 school groups now in membership. Work parties and academic courses on particular subjects have widened the contacts of ISCF for evangelism on indirect lines with increasing profit. Many of the seniors reached are humanistic or even pagan in outlook. A small but increasing proportion show interest afterwards and the potential of leadership among the converts is great. The healthy outward-looking approach of this work needs expert controlling. It is good to note that there was great profit from the Earl's Court Billy Graham Crusades, despite the fact that they were ill-timed for young people, coming at the peak examination period. The follow-up of the Crusades among school children was well prepared in advance and this has certainly paid dividends. Another point of interest to note is the problem of integration of young people into churches or groups – so many young people regard the church as a 'write-off'. In common with the other movements specializing in work among young people – Crusaders, Covenanters, Campaigners, CPAS Youth on Service – the ISCF makes a specific evangelistic thrust through a full and varied programme of camps and holiday activities.

(b) Students

At present there are 202,000 students in 32 Universities and 151 Colleges of Education, Art, and Technical Colleges. It has been estimated that by 1970 there will be 340,000 students (Robbins Report). Students form a very small proportion of society (only one for every 250 people in Britain) and yet many are the future leaders of the country and wield a greater influence than their numbers suggest. Against a background of violence and much publicized interest in sex, drugs, and humanism it is remarkable to read the recent reports of the Inter-Varsity Fellowship. Far from being on the defensive, they assert that there is a marked turning of the tide. From many Universities comes news of increasing attendance at meetings and of the greater impact of the witness of Christian Unions. The whole pattern of further education has radically altered in recent years, with many technical colleges receiving university charters, colleges of education extending their courses and seeking degree status for students, etc. Following close behind these developments comes the establishment of Christian groups and often rapid growth in the first few years of existence. The Technical Colleges Christian Fellowship and Colleges of Education Christian Union have had considerable growth. There are most encouraging signs in the latter, with 300 lecturers as associate members. It has been necessary to increase the number of IVF staff workers. The Billy Graham Crusade made most impact on these colleges, and there were a large number of conversions.

Why is the expected defeatism not present? There is a new and united strategy, under God, in student work. Graduates support it, remembering with thankfulness the earlier work in this mission field from which they benefited. The old pattern of evangelistic meetings is being replaced by regular Bible meetings, so that Christian students are truly grounded in Scripture. Though these teaching sessions are not primarily evangelistic, many individuals are drawn in as they are honest about their ignorance and want to have some explanation of the Christian Gospel. Evangelism is conducted chiefly in small groups in halls of residence, hostel rooms, or digs, and sometimes as high a proportion as two-thirds of those present at such meetings are non-Christians. But here again there is the opportunity of training for evangelism, and in this workshop setting the assistant missioner or travelling secretary can show the Christian student how not to be floored when there is a bombardment of questions. It is said that the present buoyancy of students has come through this training following on much Bible teaching.

Strategy is again apparent in the use of literature. This has long been a feature of evangelism in the student world, but it is heightened now, and more directly evangelistic. The leaflet *Sex and the Single Student* has been handed out in thousands. Many read and discuss such literature from the point of the Law at first, but later are converted through the proclamation of the Gospel.

Timing is also a part of a new strategy. In the largely non-residential colleges and universities, the lunch hours are an invaluable time for contacting non-Christian friends. A balance of activity in the unions with as much of an outward look as possible is encouraged.

In the past the link with the churches has been stronger in the South; recently there has been an encouraging linking up in the North as well. Students still exercise some responsibility outside their colleges and have a concern for overseas students and help in church campaigns in vacations. In the latter, the strategy has also altered, with house meetings often replacing the large meetings.

A new factor in the student situation, and one likely to make its presence felt increasingly, is the movement known as Campus Crusade. 'Come Help Change the World' is the slogan/title on the cover of the staff recruiting brochure of this American-based and aggressive agency, with (in 1967) a staff of 800, and ambitious plans for international expansion; already a team has been at work in England. 'Seeking to maximise their influence for Christ within the context of a group, the University Ambassador team members train for two years in the United States and then go as a group to another country to present the message of Christ to students there.' One secret of the phenomenal growth of this movement undoubtedly lies in the crisp statement of the staff brochure – 'Campus Crusade for Christ operates financially as a faith mission organization. Thus it becomes the responsibility of each staff member to raise the necessary finances for his personal ministry' (plus 20 per cent for 'overheads'). Campus Crusade does not limit itself to universities, and its department concerned with training lay men and women in evangelism may well come to the fore in England as it has already done in Australia and elsewhere.

(c) Immigrants

Information for this section was largely obtained from an existing E.A. group studying Immigration.

In 1968, according to the *Daily Telegraph* Information Service, there are in Britain some 350,000 West Indians, 250,000 immigrants from India, and 150,000 from Pakistan; there are many more from Ireland.

It is stated that today there are about 1 million immigrants in England – that is about 2% of the population. In some areas, e.g., Islington, the figure is around or over 10%. The highest estimate for 1985 is 3,500,000 as against a population of 62,000,000. This would represent 5.6%.

The E.A. Group studied the settled population of immigrants, and not overseas students. They said definitely that it is the local church which has to face the problems and find answers to this situation.

The most significant factor they discovered is that the differing ethnic groups for the main part appear to be increasing in social cohesion, and appear to be developing specific ethnic activities; with this goes a development of such institutions as West Indian churches. It may only be a temporary feature, although this is by no means certain. Prejudice and discrimination among the people of this country could cause the various ethnic groups (and especially the more 'visible' ones, such as West Indians) to withdraw even more into exclusive activities and life; and along with this will go a religious exclusiveness, including the increase in specifically ethnic group Christian churches. At the same time, the motivation for this comes as much from within such groups as from outside pressures.

Another important factor emerges – local churches in areas where there is a large population from overseas have for the most part been *conspicuously ineffective in their outreach*, and in the extent to which they have been able to bring members of other ethnic groups into their fellowship.

Separate places of worship exist for social as well as theological reasons. It is not difficult to see the reasons why this develops. 'Having not found acceptance and a congenial spiritual home in the existing churches, and as part of the general reaction to the difficulties of living in this country, such churches as these have not only arisen, but are becoming more prolific. There is a very real danger of the development of separate black and white churches.' Every effort should be made to ensure this does not develop in this country.

However, the E.A. Group state about the present situation, 'The presence of existing specific ethnic group churches should be accepted as a fact in the contemporary scene. In many ways they are fulfilling a ministry and reaching people pastorally and evangelistically *who would otherwise not* be reached.'

(d) Industry

Direct evangelism through groups associated with the Workers' Christian Fellowship and specialist bodies like 'Outreach to Industry' represents a very small factor in

British Industry as a whole. Of 26 groups of the Workers' Christian Fellowship who filled in a questionnaire, only four stated that their aim is 'outreach'. Eight said that they aimed at 'outreach and mutual spiritual help'; the rest saw 'mutual help' as their aim. Conversions are rare, and follow-up is difficult. A Stores Chaplain in the West End and an industrial evangelist agree with an industrial evangelism movement that the ultimate answer here lies in the individual Christian being enabled to see and fulfil his rôle in the setting of his daily work. Conferences on Industrial Life, organized with this in view by Christian Teamwork, have operated largely at the managerial and manager-trainee level.

(e) Business and Professional Groups

In recent years, Christian Business Men's Committees have been formed in a number of towns. These organize luncheons and dinners to which they invite their non-Christian friends and colleagues. Non-Christian but prominent professional townspeople are invited to functions when the speaker is of a similar vocation to themselves.

Even in these days of falling church attendance, professional and business men are often prepared to attend such functions and listen to the Gospel from a fellow-layman. The numbers attending luncheons average 50/60, and some 25 minutes are allowed for the after-luncheon message. The evening events are more leisurely and wives are often included in the invitations. It is found useful to have a small booklet available to remind the guests in their own homes of the things they have heard.

The Gideons is an association of Christian professional and business men. They place Bibles in what may be called the 'traffic lanes' of life: in hospitals, prisons, schools and hotels.

The Gideons commenced operations in this country in 1949, and have already placed over four million copies of the scriptures in hotels and hospitals and in the hands of school leavers, and police and nursing recruits, etc.

Many direct and indirect results flow from this work by the 99 branches in the British Isles. Above all, the Gospel is proclaimed by this means in places where it would not otherwise be heard.

Reference should also be made in this section to the effective re-deployment of inner-city churches as centres of evangelism among business and professional men. Outstanding here is St. Helen's, Bishopsgate, London, which has recently added specialist youth events to its lunch-hour and related activities. Similar developments are taking place in Bristol, Birmingham, Manchester, and other cities.

(f) Industrial Areas

Evangelicals have, until recently, fared as badly as most other Christians in their attempts to operate in the industrial inner areas of England's great cities. Such churches as have prospered have tended to be preaching centres, to which adherents have travelled considerable distances. But with the development of the Mayflower Family Centre in East London and the Toxteth Team ministry in Liverpool a change is taking place. This is being encouraged by the circulation of David Sheppard's duplicated 'Correspondence' under the title *Christians in Industrial Areas*. This is proving a highly effective medium for the exchange of ideas and experiences in what has been a desperately neglected area of society, with a clear emphasis on the need for involvement in depth, centred in a living community of Christians.

(g) Rural Areas

In the eighteenth century spiritual life was strong in the villages after the Revival and spread of Methodism. Today there are areas without any evangelical witness. East Anglia

112

appears to be better served in recent years, but the extreme North-west, North-east border counties, and parts of the West country are comparatively neglected.

The movement of population from the countryside over the past 150 years has accelerated in post-war years. In one sense there has been a movement back to the country, as housing estates have mushroomed on farmland, but those who live there are more conscious of links with the town than the surrounding country. Problems of reaching folk with the Gospel in such developing areas are being tackled, but the true countryside with an ever-dwindling population has perhaps greater problems. Comments from workers in country areas aptly describe these problems. 'Every farm has its TV since the electricity grid crossed the hills, but street lights are unknown. Who will leave his home on a wintry night to come down a muddy track to the village chapel? The youths are mechanically minded and once in their cars will go miles to the nearest cinema or coffee bar.' Already many places of worship are grouped together for one man's ministry, therefore there are no visiting, no mid-week Bible Study and no campaigns.' It is estimated in one district that 2 or 3 chapels will close within a generation. A lack of teaching of the essentials of Christian doctrine is reported. Places of worship have linked villagers and farmers socially, as well as spiritually, but now the former has assumed overall importance. In some parts the cults have invaded successfully.

An increasing impact of Baptist, Christian Brethren, and Anglican work has been noted in East Anglia. The influx of young evangelicals into the Anglican ministry has led to many taking on groups of so-called mini-parishes. This has started in East Anglia and has spread to Oxfordshire, and now to the countryside of the North-west and East. Counties Evangelistic Work has given 'society' backing to small Christian Brethren groups, and there is considerable evangelism by itinerant workers. The FIEC have set up three caravans for young couples to travel around in Wales, Dorset, and the Yorkshire Dales. The work of the Caravan Mission (Scripture Union) is comprehensive and is reaching old and the young through tent missions and similar special efforts.

Teams of young people have lately begun to go out to the countryside in holiday periods for missions. The National Young Life Campaign has a team based on York, originally involved in beach missions on the Yorkshire coast, which since 1965 has gradually extended and been consolidated in the East Yorks inland area. A committee of ten school-teachers and post-graduate workers has been behind the young people (100 in 1967) who have gone out into the villages. The number of teams is increasing. Homes are visited with literature, advertising meetings for old and young. Six weeks are spent in each place and many are re-visited. Follow-up is conducted through tapes, correspon-dence courses, news letters and occasional rallies to meet together. Bible Studies are encouraged in the homes. Simi-larly, a group of young people on holiday with the Sudan United Mission brought encouragement to an area sur-rounding Shrewsbury. In Norfolk a group of young men has been mobilized by the Covenanter Union to spend their holidays in village evangelism, in which they have co-operated closely with local churches.

Residential Schemes have been started in East Anglia. The Datchet House development provides property where Chris-tian workers may retire in order to share in the ministry of chapels and churches which are about to be closed for lack of workers and interest. These centres have brought new hope and witness to the villages assisted, and others nearby. Associates have moved in to live and share in the work, and teams of young people have also gone out from Datchet.

The Pickenham Trust is newly formed under the leadership of an Anglican vicar in Norfolk. Again, the intention is to bring together a witnessing community of believers to reinforce the message of the evangelical church. Convinced Christian teachers are now in the schools; grouping of churches allows for assistant staff and fellowship in ministry. A long-term stay is planned by the leaders of the work and a 'strategy' centre is being developed. It is hoped that a number of Christians from a variety of backgrounds will retire and give ten to twenty years of service for Christ.

The basic pattern of reaching rural areas through the revival of *churches* is further confirmed by the experiences of bodies like the Friends' Evangelistic Band.

13. MINORITIES

(a) Prisons and Related Institutions

The total population of the prisons in 1967 was some 35,000; this represents a very small proportion of the population, but special efforts have always been made to meet this need. Film evangelism is a popular method (Fact and Faith Films and Billy Graham Films, partly financed by their producers and by the E.A. Film Fund are used); the London Crusader Choir of the Elim Pentecostal Churches visits prisons most Sundays of the year; the Church Army and the Salvation Army and prison visitors all take a special interest in this field. Evangelicals have also had a big part in developing the 'Langley House' scheme for ex-prisoners, helping to cope with the problem of integration into society. Local Evangelical Fellowships in cities where prisons are located have been taking steps to co-ordinate existing activities and to inform churches as to ways in which they can help. All agree that this is not an area of evangelism for the superficial approach; careful study and understanding of the underlying socio/psychological factors are essential.

In this general area, mention should be made of the two

115

specialist staff members of the Scripture Union who visit Approved Schools and Institutions and enjoy very great opportunities for evangelism among the young people there.

(b) Drug-Taking

Registered drug addicts in 1960 were 300–400. In 1966, they were 1,139, of whom 749 were on heroin and 200 were under 20. In 1968 the figure is stated to be around 1,500, but many are unregistered as yet, and estimates are around the 3,000 mark. This is such a small section of the total population that it would not warrant separate mention – the number of alcoholics is much greater – but for the unusual degree of publicity and attention given to this area of need in evangelical circles. (This disproportionate emphasis itself calls for analysis.)

A number of specialist organizations have been set up to work in this area; evangelistic services are held in city centres, 'rehabilitation' centres are being set up in the provinces. The influence of American pentecostal organizations appears to be strong among those concerned. It is at present impossible to evaluate the work being done by comparison with other agencies. Stories of remarkable individual transformation do not provide the necessary data for objective analysis; the 'failure rate' is not so well publicized.

14. METHODS

(a) Evangelists

In this section we deal with the work of individuals and organizations specializing in direct evangelism. The definition of the gift of an evangelist is dealt with in the Theological section (chapter two). In using the term 'evangelists' in this way, we do not wish to beg the theological question as to the rôle of ministers and Christians in general in evangelism; we use it simply in its commonly understood meaning.

116

Questionnaires were sent to 100 known evangelists (there are many more itinerating, of whom details are not known); 63 were returned. Of these evangelists all but 17 were supported financially, wholly or in part, by a movement or organization of some kind; Scripture Union, for example, accounted for 13 of these. Forty-three declared themselves to be full-time evangelists (12 of these were primarily children's evangelists); most of the others combined this work with pastoral or teaching ministry. There was broad agreement on the need for Christians generally to recognize the gift and office of the evangelist, though all Christians were considered to be involved in the work of evangelism.

A question about preparation for evangelism in any given setting showed that the majority favoured a period of a year for this purpose; the encouragement of prayer was the major feature in this, along with visitation and training of Christians.

The areas of England covered by existing evangelists appear to be predominantly the South, London, and the Midlands; but this factor may be influenced by the limited basis on which the questionnaires were distributed.

A question was asked about the type of evangelism specialized in. The Scripture Union and Church Army element was removed, since their policy is centred in local church missions, and the result showed clearly that local church campaigns are by far the most usual. There is evidence, however, that financial need compels a number of evangelists to take 'one-night' bookings, and these are not by any means the best use of the evangelists' gifts – as they themselves agree.

Other answers confirmed the impression that there is a significantly greater response among young people; and that there is a small response from groups at both ends of the social scale.

Evangelists were asked about co-operating with doctrinally non-evangelical churches and individuals. Given the assurance of being free to preach as they felt right, the majority are willing to take such opportunities where they are given.

A significant number of evangelists spoke of the problems of 'integrating' converts into church life, in spite of the preponderance of local church campaigns. This should possibly be related to another general finding from this questionnaire – namely, that 'house meetings' of different kinds are the outstanding new factor in evangelism. It appears that men and women converted in such an environment are more easily integrated into the church afterwards. Some suggest that this is a desirable 'way in' regardless of how or where the actual conversion took place.

Finally, we note that five out of the sixty-three who filled in questionnaires referred to the need for national coordination in evangelism. Others spoke of areas which are seldom reached and where there is evident need. It is apparent that a lack of overall strategy in this matter is a serious lack among evangelicals. The recent national conference of evangelists, due to be repeated in December 1968, may contribute towards meeting this need – though the evidence would suggest that unless the churches are involved from the start, hopes must be limited.

(b) Societies

This is a very heterogeneous group and includes the City Missions, Salvation Army and Church Army, in addition to the many smaller groups with a specialist ministry. It also necessarily involves some overlapping with the previous section. Altogether some 35 societies filled in questionnaires. It is of interest to note that the larger societies were formed about a hundred years ago for work in the cities which were growing fast at that time. Apart from some others which were formed at the end of the last century, half of those questioned came into being in the immediate post-war years. These are either for children's work or are specifically concerned in training for evangelism. A number of the latter are imports – e.g., Navigators, Operation Mobilization, and Ambassadors for Christ. One society lamented the recent proliferation of societies and desired greater co-operation and forming of teams for evangelism. But another British society run on similar lines to an imported scheme for evangelism admits no rivalry and wished there were more groups intent on this, because of the outstanding need for training in evangelism.

The majority of the societies questioned are interdenominational and founded by groups for an evangelistic purpose. Some societies have many voluntary assistants in addition to an executive committee (usually all male) serving in a voluntary capacity. One society specializing in evangelism among young people estimates that some 3,000 voluntary helpers take part annually in its holiday activities programme.

At this point in the Report, it is appropriate to give some idea of the scale of holiday activities organized by societies which specialize in evangelism among young people. The list does not include all such societies, nor are all their activities specifically evangelistic in intent; nevertheless these activities among young people of school age – camps, houseparties, work parties, sailing cruises, overseas journeys – are an important element in evangelism in our day, and represent a considerable concentration of effort, mostly involving voluntary leadership; nor should we overlook the training processes which are built into these programmes, most of which are staffed by those who have grown up within them. The pattern of operation, with a small professional nucleus servicing and supporting a much greater team of voluntary workers, represents a highly economical and efficient use of resources.

Numbers of young people involved annually

Campaigners	1,400
Covenanter Union (Boys)	1,100
Girl Covenanters	900
Crusaders Union (Boys)	2,250
Crusaders Union (Girls Association)	700
Girl Crusaders Union	Statistics not given
Scripture Union	4,400

The above do not include denominational activities, of which the following are examples:

Church Pastoral-Aid Society (Youth on Service)	1,470
Assemblies of God (Pentecostal)	500
Elim Youth Movement	2,000
Pathfinders	2,000

In addition, a number of missionary societies have youth departments, which organize holiday activities with an evangelistic aim; for example:

Bible and Medical Missionary Fellowship	
Overseas Missionary Fellowship	85

Besides the above there is the important work done at residential holiday centres – Capernwray Hall, Herne Bay Court, Hildenborough Hall among them. These include adults as well as young people, and it is not really possible to give accurate statistical information. But the continuing witness given directly and indirectly through these agencies has a distinctive part in the total evangelistic outreach in Britain.

In the section of the questionnaire on methods of outreach, the personal approach was mentioned several times in gaining membership, but it is impossible to separate direct evangelism from the appeal for membership. Most societies have changed their methods in recent years though the aim is unchanged. The principal change has involved a decentralization which would appear to be a healthy development, allowing a more personal link and an approach more relevant to the different areas of the country.

Society representatives were not slow to make comment on evangelical churches. 'Old-fashioned approach hinders,' was a typical comment, and the tension between the society and the churches was evident in a comment from a children's society – 'Some have possessive Sunday school teachers who do not wish their children to progress,' and the more general comment on some difficulties of integration of converts. Many commented on the great shortage of workers and leaders (voluntary and full-time) and the blame was laid at the door of modern society which is also said to be responsible for the apathy and disinterest among non-believers. There was more than a hint of complacency in several answers, and one society honest enough to admit less impact over recent years had a bright new piece of literature to commend its work. Most of the literature supplied was rather dull.

Societies generally appear to fill gaps in the Church's work, give cross-links with workers in other parts of the country, and provide fellowship for isolated believers who are seeking to witness at work. Children and young people are specially catered for. Six societies admitted a dearth of the elderly, particularly males, in their membership. 'Is it right that response should dictate policy?' was the question asked by one who noticed this, and yet it seems inevitable if the society is to continue.

Societies generally supported the Billy Graham Crusades, encouraging workers to participate in counselling, etc., and usually gained membership in consequence, though this was not a deliberate policy. Almost all societies use audio-visual aids and seem to take a lead in this work. Under the heading 'major need in evangelism in England today' half stressed the need for more personal evangelism, and are prepared to give training. One interesting comment made was, 'Some Christians do not realize they are far enough on and that *they* are entrusted with the Gospel'. Is this a failure of the church with a passive congregation?

Some interesting comments on future developments have come from the London City Mission, one of the older-established societies dealing specifically in evangelism:

'Mission halls as "Poor Man's Church" are no longer necessary, but the better-equipped and staffed have a place in the strategic covering of London with evangelical places of work and witness.

'Specialist missionaries to industry etc., are more needed than ever. There is also the need for specialist missionaries to sections of the community, with particular needs such as Drug Addicts, Homeless, and the Immigrants.

'In all probability it will be necessary and desirable to reduce the number of mission halls, but to develop strategic centres as mentioned above with teams of missionaries working from these centres. It will also be desirable for more missionaries to be placed in local evangelical churches. In order to make good the reduction in the number of mission centres, it might be necessary to form mobile missions, which could be used for local open air meetings, tract distribution and Sunday schools.

'If local radio becomes available, this might well be a desirable new departure, but would necessitate recruitment of specialist staff.'

It is good to see future strategy being thought out in this way. Many societies simply said they were carrying on as in the past.

As an outcome of the preceding, we asked five people who are deeply involved in evangelism among young people some questions: Do young people respond most freely? Or is it that most work is done among them? The older generation is not reached – is it because they are 'hard'? or because they are neglected? Here are their answers:

David Winter: 'Young people are more open, more pliable, less in a rut, so evangelism in this group is more rewarding and therefore more work is done here. This seems to me logical and right (Acts 18.6); you don't keep hammering on closed doors!'

Verna Wright: 'There are more socially organized groups for them . . . being unattached they are more easily reachable. Rallies usually attract Christians only in the older age bracket. House meetings do attract young people. Older folk are harder to reach (they have many commitments), but they are not unreachable. House meetings are effective. We have many activities at beach missions as part of a strategy to win parents. Special events at churches can be followed up by diligent visiting. Crusades give talking point with older generation – they are more likely to come to Crusade meetings than other meetings.'

Kenneth Habershon: 'I agree that most of the work is done among young people, and most response is obtained from them. They are not so hardened to sin; idealism and desire for truth are characteristic. Work among middle-aged and elderly is neglected, particularly the aspect of fellowship, so strong among young people, and necessary as a spearhead for evangelism. Formality and tradition have hindered work among adults. Do we know of adults hindered in the past by what was done when they were younger?'

David Sheppard: 'Our church work is unbalanced in favour of children's and young people's work. We have abandoned the faith that God can bring adults to Himself. We tend to view the church like a pyramid – many coming in as children, some survive to adulthood. We ought to believe in additions at all ages. Young people go to rallies

123

and respond in numbers, but adults sit tight – they make decisions in small groups or through personal work. This is a reflection on our church life.'

Michael Eastman: 'This needs much further investigation in depth. We might discover that the current strategy of evangelism is misdirected. We should remember the characteristics of adolescence – conversions can be as ephemeral as adolescent love affairs, and as susceptible to religious exploitation as commercial exploitation. Have these young people survived later pressures (taking up jobs, marriage, raising children, etc.), and do they remain effective Christians in fellowship with a local group of believers? This is a different question, but a more relevant one. Nevertheless this is an age in which values are formed and it is an age to appeal to. The growth of a teenage subculture points to the need for special forms of evangelism.'

By way of a general summary of this section, and bearing in mind the special problems created in the area of relationships between the societies and the churches, we would make the following comments.

To judge from the statistics we should find the churches bulging with young marrieds. But we do not. A considerable percentage of the nation's children are in Sunday school and yet the toughest job seems to be the integration of young people into churches. We have the paradox of evangelists setting their sights on young people because the churches are not catering for them. This lack of flexibility may also be reflected in lack of real response amongst men and old people. To be effectively 'making disciples' is too demanding. So we have 'church substitutes', coffee-bars for the young, special fellowships for women, and little or nothing for men. Maybe we have not thought and prayed creatively over the real needs of people, nor met them at the point of their need. Concentration on young people may also conceal an implicit loss of nerve – it is easy to deal with those less knowledgeable. We also note the increasing sophistication of teenagers. So we go to younger ones, before the problem begins. Is this an unconscious admission of defeat by the churches in yet another area?

(c) House Groups

House meetings are on the increase, and are found all over the country. They appear to meet the need of all types of person. It is possible to divide them generally into two types. Those used for evangelism are often large, and may spread from a home to a restaurant or even a university refectory, while Bible study and prayer meetings are generally smaller and more stable. The former attract those who would never enter a church. The Bible study meeting is used for the building up of those thus converted and forms the link between the open evangelistic gathering and church attendance and membership. Some house meetings have grown up where there is no evangelistic witness or where there is dissatisfaction over the failure of the church to communicate the Gospel.

In many cases the house meeting provides a fellowship and caring atmosphere often lacking in the formal church set-up, and even where churches have only got as far as introducing the prayer meeting to members' homes, there has often been a growth in the meeting and a greater reality in prayer for the neighbourhood. It is heartwarming to hear of homes opened for the care and evangelism of the misfits of society, who perhaps have never had a home before and now, thoroughly institutionalized, have only a hostel – another institution – to go to. An interesting feature of Dr. Eileen Frankland's meetings in Pudsey, or those run in connection with the Stewards' Trust, is the link, a natural and easy one, forged through meeting folk in the course of work. Need becomes evident and a simple invitation to the home afterwards allows for easy evangelism. Again, the type of meeting over a meal affords a natural and uncontrived setting for sharing the gospel and is not contrived.

The most successful home meetings seem to be those run for women and young people. In a sense, the small group invited by a woman to her home is nothing new, yet the woman with time during the day to invite the lonely ones – e.g., those who have moved out of the towns and away from their families – can bring much social as well as spiritual benefit to her neighbours. Children's meetings have often replaced the Sunday school, especially where families go out together for the Sunday in the country or by the sea. Men will go to meetings with their wives or will have a meeting in the home organized by the wife, but it appears that men's meetings generally have a venue other than the home. Young people's evangelism has capitalized on recreation for some years. Courage and imagination is now needed to do this for men.

Studying different house meetings it is evident that those with a threefold strategy – linking home, church, and work – are thriving, with the possibility of continuous evangelism avoiding the strain of seizing just the brief period of a camp or rally. Those who open their homes have the opportunity of proclaiming the Gospel (either themselves, or by asking someone else, perhaps an expert in another field), of studying and discussing the application of Scripture, of caring for the less fortunate and giving in the easiest and most natural way. At work they find themselves in a mission field where their lives are under constant surveillance but where they rub shoulders with many non-Christians. The church should form the outlet for worship of those invited to the home, and provide cross-links of fellowship with other home groups, preventing cliques and complacency.

Three churches with this pattern can be examined. One group has an emphasis on cell growth. Two leaders are training up two others to be ready for a split-off when the Bible study group has grown from 8 to 15. Each cell is represented on a guiding committee which meets to plan evangelistic meetings and weekends, and each guiding committee is represented on a steering committee. New members of Bible study sets are contacted in the City and the groups provide fellowship and opportunities for evangelism for those who 'weekend' and worship out of London. The Mayflower Centre encourages Christian couples to invite home those met at work, out shopping, or in the Centre's recreation clubs. The strong leadership from the church and the help given to young couples by the housing association to stay in the district fosters this sort of outreach. St. Barnabas, Cray, has evolved a house meeting style of evangelism to meet the need of a GLC (Council) estate. 13 house groups under the vicar's supervision bring in many neighbours in need, and work-mates interested in a Gospel that works. These three are evangelizing the neglected upper and lower classes. Two final points: home meetings are on the increase since folk move around so much these days. They can be a means of breaking new ground as people who have been helped move on and desire to start their own, which may prove the nucleus of a church. Secondly, their value in keeping church people together and active, and the teaching possibilities can make for training in leadership and ensure continuity in a work for Christ.

15. MASS MEDIA

(a) Radio/Television

The pattern of control of radio and television in Britain is unique in the world. Visitors from overseas, particularly from America, where commercialism reigns supreme in a cultural desert of directly sponsored programmes with few oases, find it hard to comprehend. Some British Evangelicals, with understandable enthusiasm, pin their hopes on the adoption of commercially sponsored radio in Britain. The idea of being able to buy time is very attractive – to those who have the money. But as the brief encounter with pirate radio revealed, among those with ample supplies of money are American cults and sects ranging from Herbert Armstrong to 'Frank and Ernest' of the Jehovah's Witnesses. Those who have listened to the babel of religious programmes in California have been known to change their opinion about the BBC on their return!

We must therefore look at the situation as it is, and try to evaluate its significance for evangelism. Direct broadcasting from 'missionary' radio stations to Britain is virtually limited to Radio Monte Carlo, a good deal of which is on the short wave band, and very hard to receive satisfactorily. In spite of the occasional remarkable conversion story, it must be assumed that broadcasts from this station mainly reach the converted who are prepared to take the trouble to locate the programme and listen through the background noises.

The BBC's responsibility is to reflect the life of the churches of all varieties; Evangelicals have to take their turn, and evangelism of a direct kind is rare. Penry Jones, Head of BBC Religious Broadcasting, defines its aims as threefold – to provide worship of a high quality for churchgoers; to provide information and the most recent theological thinking for the community at large; and to have a genuine concern with those on the fringes of, or totally outside, the Christian Church. As an example of the latter category, which is nearest to an evangelistic concern, there were 14 million who listened to 'Five to Ten' (BBC Radio) once or twice a week. Three million watch 'Meeting Point' (BBC TV).

Asked 'What place does evangelism have in broadcasting?', Penry Jones replied, 'To be heard in a living room at the courtesy of the listener or viewer means first of all

128

that one has to converse rather than orate. Secondly, what one has to say must attract their attention and it must have some meaning for them; they must be prepared to go on listening to what one is saying. I would have thought it is a bad medium therefore for propaganda, and that it would be wrong to use it for proselytizing in any sense, because it is a public medium . . . This doesn't mean that broadcasting should not be evangelistic. It just means that you have to broaden your interpretation of what you mean by evangelistic. Religious broadcasting should be concerned with proclamation, and the question appropriate to radio or appropriate to television. That is basic.' (This information comes from an interview with Penry Jones reported on by the Radio/TV correspondent of *The Christian*, issue of May 31, 1968.)

Evangelicals with some experience of broadcasting speak of a large measure of freedom. One who took a series of the 'People's Service' programme reported that the BBC were happy for him to be as evangelistic as he wished, to include a prayer of personal commitment to Christ, and the offer of a booklet about personal faith in Christ; some 1,600 letters were received in response.

Another writes, 'I doubt if it is very good theology to expect other people normally to be converted to Christ sitting in their armchairs at home. I know this sometimes happens because the Holy Spirit is not bound by rules. The normal place for the preaching of the Gospel in the New Testament is when people have continuing relationships or the possibility of them with individual Christians or a Christian group . . . one of the two great purposes of religious broadcasting should be to do a good public relations job for the Christian Church, because our object ought to be to get people out of their armchairs and into the company of effective Christians . . . The second great purpose is, I believe, to keep or strengthen people's consciousness of God whether they are committed Christians or not.'

The same writer emphasizes what others who are actually involved say – 'We need to work hard to use the media as best we can ... We often sit round complaining we are not given opportunities. What I believe we should be doing is to get people we know who can write good scripts to do this, and keep submitting them.'

The other obvious way of constructive action is to encourage young people to make a career in radio and television, or in journalism, to master the relevant creative skills in art and literature, and to equip themselves for positions of responsibility in the great mass media organizations of our time. This is long-term, undramatic, work, but must be taken seriously, as it is by the Roman Catholics.

(b) Literature

What follows is based largely on a report submitted by the Publications Secretary of the Church Pastoral-Aid Society; here again it is almost impossible to give anything like a complete picture of what is going on.

(i) *General Comments:* There may be little evidence for 'literature evangelism' in the New Testament (although Philip made good use of the MSS in the Ethiopian Eunuch's possession) but the only reason that we know anything of Christ and the first Christians is that people *wrote* about them!

If Marshall McLuhan is right, we are approaching a situation where men are more inclined to respond to media than present material with immediacy, in patchwork-quilt style, rather than with organized, mathematical, logical sequence. One could say that print is thereby ruled out and that the Church cannot rely heavily upon it.

A study of the national press (Britain's is a great newspaper-reading culture) and literature-advertising in the secular world reveals very quickly that those in commerce who have vital interests in communicating information are far from abandoning the printed page. What they have abandoned, however, is the reliance on typeface alone to communicate. Immediacy is imparted by the news photograph, diagram, or line drawing.

In the field of newspapers the *Daily Mirror* has been leading the way in employing these principles of communication. For some years the formula evolved by the *Daily Mirror* has been copied deliberately by *Challenge*, a monthly tabloid with an avowed evangelistic aim. The high circulation of *Challenge* (over 200,000) reveals that it has the confidence of many Christians anxious to distribute literature. Here is a piece of literature that attempts to convey its message in a way that requires the minimum of mental adaptation from the reader. The use of photograph, headline, opening digest paragraph, cross-headings, short sentences and short paragraphs, and the maximum play on human interest is backed by high quality producing and imaginative editorial.

Another venture attempting to use the *Daily Mirror* formula is *The Leader*, published in the North West. The great advantages here are the facilities available for localizing, so that the paper can become a tool genuinely related to an identifiable local group of people – some church or group of churches. There is considerable value in localizing as the experiment with an adaptation of *The Leader* in Everton has convincingly shown. There is a considerable public-relations function in such a paper at a time when the church in an impersonal urban district needs to consider that matter very carefully.

In an entirely different field of literature we have the booklets devised by David Sheppard and published by Scripture Union. These are the most serious and deliberate attempt yet in the field of Christian literature to present the

Gospel by means of a modern understanding of the use of print. The coolest form of communication is the conversation within a natural group. These booklets attempt to take you inside such a group inviting (implicitly rather than explicitly) the reader to learn casually as the group discovers things. It is too early to say whether the booklets have succeeded – sales figures, although high, are not an adequate guide. Christian literature needed the advent of this experiment, and it is probable that there would be no way to get the wisdom needed other than 'wisdom after the event'.

All this points to the importance not only of seeing what is needed in the field of literature concepts, but the expertise to execute these concepts. This is a field for the professional, and the Church cannot afford to rely on enthusiastic amateurs when it comes to typographical design.

(ii) *Books:* There is no scarcity of evangelical book publishing. The last five years have seen a revolution in this field. In addition to a high output from commercial publishers like Hodder & Stoughton and William Collins – much of which is valuable for evangelical and even evangelistic purposes–'branded' publishing concerns such as Scripture Union, IVF, Falcon Books, Victory Press, Marshall, Morgan and Scott, Paternoster, Pickering and Inglis, Banner of Truth and others have stepped up book production and greatly improved quality of presentation.

While this is heartening to the Christian, there are also some real causes for anxiety. All these organizations expect their overall publishing programmes to be self-supporting. There is nothing necessarily un-Christian about this, but as it works out in practice one must ask whether commercial viability does not over-ride the concerns of ministry.

The people who are buying popular Christian literature have, usually, two things in common. First, they are already Christians. Secondly, they are middle class. The purely evangelistic impact of popular Christian literature is desperately small. Further, the outreach resulting from much creative and expensive effort by-passes almost completely the working classes and the intelligentsia.

It can be argued that books will never reach the working classes anyway, particularly in the TV age. This is probably near the truth. But when the factory worker gets converted, or even starts seeking, he may well be prepared to go further than at-a-glance booklets, and there is little to offer him that is not firmly based on the assumption that the reader comes from a semi-detached-suburbia culture.

The lack of material for the intelligentsia is serious, for the creative thoughts of one generation of intellectuals become the background assumptions of the working classes of the next generation. With the electric speed of TV this transference of thought-forms and values may well be speeded up.

A gap has been left by the death of C. S. Lewis which has not yet been filled. The IVF and Hodder & Stoughton books by Francis Schaeffer are a step in the right direction.

The opportunities offered by the secular publishing house in this area of opinion-forming pre-evangelism are immense. They offer distribution and publicity facilities that no Christian publishers can match. Christians need to pray intelligently with this in mind, and the evangelical publisher should be prepared to hand on such authors as have big market potential to those who can guarantee the big market.

Quite clearly there is a need for evangelical publishers to consult more closely. This does not mean that one great evangelical publishing house would be a desirable alternative. What is needed is consultation to avoid a too-close overlapping of projects and co-operation on some projects that a single publishing house could not handle alone.

Where there would indeed be much to gain from joint action is in the field of distribution. In Australia there is the evangelical distribution co-operative Emu, in which several doctrinally aligned publishing houses have all their distribution handled by a separate concern which offers representation facilities far beyond their individual capacities to sustain.

The question of distribution on a commercial basis also bedevils the cause of evangelism through literature. The publisher cannot be expected to be the retailer *and* seller of his goods. He has to work therefore through retailers who have to make a living out of their activity. This means that the retailer must have his percentage. When this is coupled to the fact of small print orders when compared with secular literature, the resultant prices compare very unfavourably with non-religious publishing, particularly in the paperback area. Things are made even more difficult with regard to smaller (booklet and leaflet) publications. The middle-man's 'cut' makes the price of leaflets prohibitive to many of those who would like to buy in some quantity for free distribution in evangelistic work. It must be stated, however, that the Christian public and Christian publishers owe a very great debt to Christian bookshops all over the country. Many of the proprietors of these shops are operating on pitifully small profit margins, and are kept going only by a real sense of vocation and mission.

With a personal means of communication there is comparatively little difficulty in judging effectiveness. In person-to-person communication, a man knows where he stands. With literature this is not so. The publisher of Christian literature can have no satisfaction in sales figures. They may be gratifying, but what he needs to know is not whether his books are selling, but to whom, whether they are being read, and whether they are being helpful to the reader.

It would seem, therefore, that there is a real need for some form of consumer research. It is quite conceivable that such research could show that evangelical publishers are misusing their funds, their energies, and their time to a quite significant degree. We don't know, and we shall never know – without research. On the positive side, such research could well provide information that would improve the effectiveness of future publications.

One area of literature sadly neglected by Evangelicals is the novel. Most Christian fiction of the kind available in evangelical bookshops is not in the literary class of much modern fiction; nor does it have the integrity and depth of perception which mark the best contemporary writing. As an art form it is not easy to master, and here, as in radio and television, hard work and patient training are called for. Yet millions of volumes of fiction are circulated every year – the public library could be a distribution agency for positive literature, if it could be produced.

16. CRUSADES

Some British evangelists are deeply involved in what has come to be called 'Crusade' evangelism, and there is reference to this in the earlier sections on Evangelists and Societies. But since Harringay in 1954, Crusade evangelism has come to be commonly associated with the activities of the Billy Graham Evangelistic Association, and a report of this kind must give special attention to such Crusades; in one sense they have dominated the evangelistic scene in Britain since 1954.

Here again, as always in this matter of evangelism, we face a very difficult problem of evaluation. Much of the evidence is partial and contradictory. People form strong impressions, and opinion becomes substituted for fact. Large organizations speak with different voices through different spokesmen. Where a strong sense of mission confronts great frustration, any area of hope quickly becomes a launch-pad for fantasy.

We assume that the way a Billy Graham Crusade operates is familiar to all, and that the kind of statistics issued by

Friday, June 23rd.

	Attendance	Decisions	%
London	16,500	650	3·9
TV Relays	39,920	1,043	2·6
Land line Relays	—	—	
Total	56,420	1,693	3·0

Saturday, June 24th.

	Attendance	Decisions	%
London	19,000	774	4·1
TV Relays	46,001	1,191	2·6
Land line Relays	Nil	Nil	
Total	65,001	1,965	3·0

Sunday, June 25th.

	Attendance	Decisions	%
London	14,000	619	4·4
TV Relays	48,761	1,654	3·4
Land line Relays	Nil	Nil	
Total	62,761	2,273	3·6

Monday, June 26th.

	Attendance	Decisions	%
London	20,500	619	3·0
TV Relays	58,461	1,813	3·2
Land line Relays	2,813	22	0·8
Total	81,774	2,454	3·0

Tuesday, June 27th.

	Attendance	Decisions	%
London	27,500	1,789	6·5
TV Relays	77,350	5,023	6·5
Land line Relays	3,224	68	2·1
Total	108,074	6,880	6·4

Wednesday, June 28th.

	Attendance	Decisions	%
London	24,500	845	3·5
TV Relays	66,871	1,958	2·9
Land line Relays	2,960	26	0·9
Total	94,331	2,829	3·0

Thursday, June 29th.

	Attendance	Decisions	%
London	28,500	1,926	6·7
TV Relays	78,700	6,025	7·7
Land line Relays	111,668	8,076	7·2
Total	218,868	16,027	3·0

Friday, June 30th.

	Attendance	Decisions	%
London	24,000	1,200	5·0
TV Relays	78,750	5,836	
	(Estimated)	(Estimated)	7·4
Land line Relays	4,154	64	1·5
Total	106,904	7,100	6·6

Saturday, July 1st.

	Attendance	Decisions	%
London	25,000	1,408	5·6
TV Relays	66,380	2,738	4·1
	(Estimated)	(Estimated)	
Land line Relays	4,089	69	1·7
Total	95,469	4,215	4·4

the organizers are likewise well known. For the record, here is a tabulated summary of statistics in connection with the Earl's Court/All Britain Crusade of 1967.

(Tuesday and Thursday were 'Youth Nights', featuring Cliff Richard.)

There is the familiar problem of estimating attendances, though in the case of many of the meetings referred to, careful checking was possible.

A press release issued in February 1967, and relating to the 1966 Crusade, said that a questionnaire filled in by 'a cross-section of 1,195 enquirers of the previous June's Greater London Crusade' had revealed, among other things, that:

458 said that before the Crusade they did not attend church regularly, but they now do. 658 stated they had previously attended Church regularly.

This suggests that out of 1,195 enquirers, only 79 (1,195 minus 458-plus-658) do not now attend Church. But how was the 'cross-section obtained? Inquirers who attended a follow-up meeting at the Albert Hall seven months after the Crusade were asked to pick up a questionnaire at the doors and then return it by post.

Thus a three-stage selection process meant that the forms returned came from a very special group, not in any way a 'cross-section' in the strict sense of the term. All that the figures tell us is something about a particular element in the whole spectrum of enquirers. The Billy Graham Organization did not draw the deduction above from the figures, and wisely limited itself to stating the results of the enquiry.

It was our original intention to conduct statistical research based on a random sample of enquirers' cards, and the officials of the Billy Graham Organization were ready to co-operate in this; but we agreed that in view of a pledge made after the 1956 Crusades it would not be right to intrude upon the privacy of records, and so did not proceed with this plan.

One way of examining the results of such Crusades is to make inquiries of churches in the Greater London area which were in some degree involved in the Crusade. A card index of such churches used in connection with referrals of inquirers provided the basis of this inquiry. As the answers indicated, the churches ranged from those with a slight interest to those which were enthusiastically involved. Allowance has to be made for the incorporation in the sample of one large Anglican church in the Earl's Court Area which gave very active support, and which received a large number of referrals from a typical transients' residential area in its vicinity. The inquiry related to 1966 and 1967, though some answers dealt with only one of those years.

A letter was sent to a 1 in 10 sample of the churches on the card index. The sample was representative in terms of denomination and geographical location. Eighty-five churches returned completed forms, as follows:

Both years: 53 ⎫
1966 only: 11 ⎪ 1966: 64
1967 only: 15 ⎬ 1967: 68 (+6)
One year (unspecified): 6 ⎭

For the purposes of this report, forms pertaining to an unspecified year have been taken to be for 1967. The churches were distributed through the denominations in this way:

Anglican	25	Congregational	5
Baptist	25	Pentecostal	2
Independent	17	Brethren	2
Methodist	9		

Not all the churches were firm supporters of the crusade. Twelve in 1966 and 20 in 1967 did not enrol as 'supporting churches'. It was plain from responses, too, that some had little or no sympathy with the aims and methods of the endeavour. 'It is rather unfortunate,' wrote one, 'that this church has come up in your sample as having showed initial interest . . . We simply gave certain information when re-

	1966		1967	
	Anglicans	*Others*	*Anglicans*	*Others*
All inquirers	530 (100%)	322 (100%)	211 (100%)	199 (100%)
Constitution of sample				
Adult men	82 (16%)	32 (10%)	42 (20%)	17 (9%)
Adult women	110 (21%)	42 (13%)	54 (26%)	37 (19%)
Boys (under 21)	127 (24%)	64 (20%)	42 (20%)	53 (27%)
Girls (under 21)	197 (37%)	186 (58%)	73 (35%)	96 (48%)
Not known	14 (3%)	Minus 2	—	Minus 3
Nature of Response				
Decision for Christ	335 (63%)	210 (65%)	128 (61%)	116 (58%)
Consecration	20 (4%)	20 (6%)	7 (3%)	16 (8%)
Rededication	79 (15%)	53 (17%)	45 (21%)	47 (24%)
Assurance	4 (1%)	—	3 (1%)	1
No commitment	54 (10%)	19 (6%)	22 (10%)	9 (5%)
Not known	38 (7%)	20 (6%)	6 (3%)	10 (5%)

	1966		1967	
	Anglicans	Others	Anglicans	Others
All inquirers	530 (100%)	322 (100%)	211 (100%)	199 (100%)
Church Relationship and Follow-up				
Previous contact with church	205 (39%)	175 (54%)	92 (44%)	105 (53%)
Known to have completed follow-up programme*	43 (8%)	103 (32%)	28 (13%)	36 (18%)
In regular fellowship with church at time of inquiry	123 (23%)	109 (34%)	64 (30%)	88 (44%)
In regular fellowship with another church at time of inquiry	43 (8%)	20 (6%)	19 (9%)	21 (11%)
Wanted no further contact after Crusade	57 (11%)	54 (17%)	14 (7%)	32 (16%)

* It was evident that most churches did not know how many of their inquirers had completed the follow-up programme, nor indeed whether they were now in fellowship with another church. Many churches left this particular question unanswered.

Note that these figures are particularly weighted because a local church, as far as Earl's Court is concerned, was included in the sample. 149 inquirers in 1966 and 73 in 1967 were referred there, the majority being adult, in both years.

141

quested.' It should be said that this indicates a representative cross-section since many churches did feel that way about the Crusade.

The returns account for 852 enquirers in 1966 and under half of that number, 410, in 1967. This may be because the card index was made up of churches in Greater London, to which the 1966 crusade was specifically aimed. We cannot take this as being a good sample of inquirers, because they were by no means well distributed among the churches. Over half the 1966 inquirers arise from the returns from only seven churches. They were distributed as shown below.

Churches were asked how they dealt with inquirers. This table shows how many of the inquirers were visited by the minister in the various churches.

	Anglican	Others
All inquirers	16 (64%)	29 (47%)
Most inquirers	4 (16%)	14 (23%)
Some inquirers	3 (12%)	3 (5%)
None of the inquirers	—	5 (8%)
No reply	2 (8%)	10 (17%)

The remaining inquirers were visited by church members and trained workers. In only two churches were they approached by correspondence only. Eleven of the churches did nothing further if inquirers did not respond to their first approach, in some or all cases. One Anglican church with a large number of inquirers adopted this policy in 1967 as a result of the lessons of 1966.

Eighteen churches said that they had problems from inadequate counselling in 1966, and 12 in 1967.

Many churches added additional comments. These were about problems from counselling (11), mass evangelism generally (10), complaints about wrong referring of inquirers (13), validation or invalidation of the Crusade by seeing what happened to inquirers (8), the situation within the church with reference to the Crusade (3), and other things not relevant to the inquiry.

The comments about counselling mostly suggested that counsellors had failed to grasp the situation of the inquirer to whom they were talking. There were cases of young people who went up to support friends, but had been recorded as having made decisions. Elsewhere decisions were recorded for people with insufficient grasp of what was involved.

On mass evangelism generally, the recurring theme was that the crusade did not make a lasting effect on the complete outsider. Even when they went, they either made no response, or made no lasting response. A belief in locally based evangelism, particularly for younger people, came out repeatedly.

The complaints that inquirers had been wrongly referred were mainly from Anglicans. Many of these were embarrassed by having been sent names of folk outside their parishes. A large number (according to the receiving church) of Roman Catholics were referred to an independent church.

Where churches made comments about the progress of inquirers as an indication of the validity of the crusade, they bore out the views expressed by others regarding mass evangelism generally. Church members, whether they went forward for any reason or not, found blessing and encouragement from the services, but the complete outsider tended to go back outside again. In the words of one comment, 'If they asked "What shall we do?" they seem to have been given little answer beyond "to decide for Christ" … On inquiry they were unable to give any real answer as to what this meant, other than that they desired to live a better life. They saw no connection between that and what they had done, except that by going forward they'd given expression to that desire.'

Television Relays were a prominent feature of the 1967

Earl's Court Crusade, and some research has been done into this particular aspect of the outreach.

At the Merseyside TV relay, there were some 1,900 'inquirers', of whom some 1,400 were in the 11–18 age group. After three months, special forms were sent to the 450 over 18s. One hundred and fifty of the 450 were returned, and in each case the report was favourable; but this method of inquiry tells us nothing about that most important group – the remaining 300. The local committee noted that of some 1,800 ministers' follow-up slips sent out, some 400 were never returned.

At Poole and Bournemouth an unusually careful and thorough follow-up system was devised, specially designed to link inquirers with accessible and sympathetic individuals and groups. For example, follow-up literature was not distributed through the post subsequent to the Relay, but delivered personally by the Counsellor when he or she felt the time was ripe. A further report on a green card was asked for four months after the Relay.

Six hundred and thirty inquirers were registered at the time of the Relays; at the meeting at which the green cards were reviewed, four and a half months after, some 308 cards were considered. The missing cards can be accounted for in several ways, mostly the result of personal failure to operate the scheme properly on the part of the Counsellors and others involved.

The green card gave information about the progress being made by the inquirer in a number of ways; it included 'My contact with the inquirer is satisfactory/unsatisfactory', which was not always rightly interpreted by the Counsellor. However, cross-checking revealed that the errors were only in the direction of declaring the relationship 'unsatisfactory' when the other factors indicated the opposite, and there was also further checking by the Area Chairman. The results were considered very encouraging.

Green Cards	'Satisfactory'	'Unsatisfactory'	Static
308	215 (69·9%)	72	1

Uncertain	Difficult	Moved Away
15	3	2

It was not possible to say how far these results were the outcome of the special follow-up procedures, but they obviously had some effect.

In general, the Commission noted that Crusades of this kind make an impression predominantly on young people, and within that age-group on a significantly higher proportion of girls than boys. Their impact on the section of the community which is normally untouched by the churches is hard to measure, and opinions differ. The nature of the impact made by such large meetings and the need for the message to be addressed primarily to a general audience made the Commission look with concern at the percentages of children of twelve and under who responded to the appeal.

17. TELEPHONE MINISTRY

In a number of ways, Christians with a concern for people in need have devised ways of using contemporary methods to contact them. One of the most notable is the spread of the Telephone Counselling idea in various forms, many of which have a direct evangelistic ministry.

The work in London was pioneered in Greenwich and has since spread to Richmond. The newest development is amongst a group of ministers in the Medway towns. Agencies exist in Liverpool, Bristol, Bournemouth, Norwich and Manchester. Parallels exist on the Continent and notably in Zurich (Switzerland). The Christian Counsel Telephone Service was founded in 1959.

An easily memorised phone number (GRE 1212) and the slogan 'Have you a problem too big to handle alone?' prominently displayed in tube trains and in the windows of counsellors and friends, have brought in innumerable inquiries, particularly on marital problems. St. Martin-in-the-Fields and the Salvation Army Goodwill work link the CCTS with those in need. The Fishers' Fellowship course is used for those converted, perhaps after long contact with the couple leading this work, and F.F. also provide a course in advanced counselling for any who come in to share in the work. Greenwich has affiliation with Halford House, Richmond, where the whole church is involved in a telephone pastorate. A similar kind of scheme is operated by the Leicester Evangelical Council.

The recording of messages to be heard by those who ring is a recent development of the Telephone Church in Manchester, where there is a team of City Missioners, denominational ministers, senior laymen and two women workers. In the Medway towns the recorded two-minute messages of a team of ten ministers are the basis of the work begun this year. A GPO answering machine has been installed in the home of a layman who changes the tapes each day. Any who require counselling are directed to an interdenominational bookshop in Chatham. It is not possible to state the number of calls in the Medway area, but the Manchester centre now has 50 calls a day, a few being for personal counselling given by a service manned 14 hours a day (compare 359 calls a day in Zurich). The Scripture Union 'Lifeline' scheme in Glasgow gives a recorded Bible reading plus comment and prayer, changed daily.

The significant factors in this evangelism include the strong sense of calling on the part of the counsellors, the prayer backing and giving of many friends, a large advisory council, usually interdenominational, the use of modern techniques – GPO machines, advertisements in tubes, on the back of buses, unusual hand-out leaflets – an understanding of the complex social problems of the day, coupled with a conviction that Christ is the only answer, and a desire to follow up those who come to faith in Him with help in Bible study.

18. MUSIC GROUPS

A phenomenon of recent years has been the way that young Christians have formed music groups of the kind popular among young people generally. They arose spontaneously as an expression of Christian faith and mostly have a lively evangelistic concern.

Seventy gospel music groups replied to a questionnaire sent out by the Commission; 59 of them are still in action and their replies are analysed. Most play a variety of music, but beat seems to be the favourite.

Thirty per cent of groups include no one older than 21. Only 23% include someone over 25. Some would urge us to point out that these young people live a dangerous Christian life, because of their immaturity and the glamour of the work in which they engage.

Asked where they operate principally, they replied:

North East:	1	*East Anglia*:	10 (16%)
North West:	15 (25%)	London:	5 (8%)
Midlands:	4 (7%)	South:	2
West Country:	6 (10%)	London & South:	9 (15%)
		No special area:	7

They seem to be strongest in areas where evangelists of the more orthodox variety are not so active, namely the North West and East Anglia.

The groups work in a great variety of places, including: open-air; reform and approved schools; youth clubs; schools; coffee bars; prisons; beat clubs; working men's clubs; colleges; dance halls; pubs; hospitals; old people's homes; night clubs; children's homes; charity shows, etc. – in fact wherever they can. Only five groups never play in secular establishments. Only eight groups have more than six bookings a month on average.

The value of their equipment, including transport (in some cases), amounted to about £500 in 30% of the groups.

Over half the groups said they either make no direct evangelistic appeal, or work in a situation where this responsibility is not theirs. For the rest, the favourite form of appeal was an invitation to stay and talk informally with the group, though ten of the groups, whether habitually or occasionally, asked people to raise their hands or come forward.

Twenty-three (40%) reckon to do follow-up by correspondence. Five of them use a course, either their own or the Fishers' Fellowship. The rest claim that this too was not their responsibility, but that of the host church or organization.

None of the groups declared themselves unwilling to co-operate with non-evangelicals, though many added the rather crucial proviso – 'provided we can make things go our way'. However, from the way they write they seem to have little trouble about this. We note the significance of this statement in the light of what is said about follow-up.

Two new groups had started a question-time during the meetings and another group sent out tapes of its songs.

The formation of Musical Gospel Outreach with its lively magazine *Buzz* is providing a focus of interest and exchange of experience which can do nothing but good in channelling the evident enthusiasm of the groups.

Though the debate on the use of modern gospel music in evangelism lingers on, it is clear such music has become widely accepted. The following comments, therefore, are intended not to add to the arguments of either side, but as constructive criticisms put forward to make the use of this medium more effective.

After some research it seems evident that many Christians, including Gospel groups, are still vague as to the rôle of modern gospel music within evangelism. Such vagueness inevitably leads to misuse, abuse, and thus confusion.

Musical Gospel Outreach, an organization active in encouraging, training, and co-ordinating those who use this medium, were asked to define the aim of modern gospel music. Their reply was:

'Modern gospel music, as well as being a vehicle for communicating the Gospel, prepares the ground for further "intense" evangelism (personal conversation, etc.). It is a tool for use in genuine outreach and can lead to opportunities and earn the user the right to speak personally.'

With the above definition in mind, one feels that modern Gospel music groups should ask themselves two questions:
(1) Is their music really an aid to their evangelism, or are they just hiding behind their guitars?
(2) Are they in fact really reaching non-Christians, or are they only entertaining Christians?

It is only fair to point out that churches who have such groups in their ranks have failed in some instances to incorporate them as a part of their evangelistic programme (this may be because so few churches have any outreach into the secular world).

A strong recommendation is that groups do outreach work in the area local to their church in order that the church as a whole may participate prayerfully; that the group may just be a part of a larger more effective team of young people, and that follow-up work may be done more adequately (i.e., personally).

Widespread criticism concerning the use of modern gospel music revolves around the poor standard of songs used by the groups. From a limited survey carried out to help the writing of this report, the songs submitted showed that the criticism, on the whole, is justified.

One feels the reason for the defects lies simply in the fact that the writers of the songs are normally group members,

149

and are therefore young people with obviously limited Christian experience and teaching, and whilst one admires and even applauds their desire to write songs their contemporaries understand, it is these limitations which tend to restrict the message in song.

A positive step to overcome this problem could be to seek out and commission mature Christians with song-writing ability (preferably with an understanding of the current pop scene), who will write songs for groups to use. Such songs, in modern English, could then be collated and added to good songs written by groups and then distributed to those who need material.

19. COFFEE BAR EVANGELISM

Here is another sign of the ability of the younger generation of Evangelicals to find contemporary ways of sharing their faith. In this section we rely very much on a piece of research carried out by Above Bar Church, Southampton, and involving a number of Christian coffee bars. Most of them consider that church premises are a disadvantage, and hire other facilities. Experience suggests that a one-night effort is of little use, but best results follow opening for a stated and limited period.

Few are self-supporting – 74% rely on donations, even though most of the workers give their services free. Licences are needed if they keep open after 10 p.m., and problems arise with drug-pushers and alcoholics – experience is the desirable factor here.

Ninety-two per cent have speakers who are allowed 5–15 minutes, up to four times a night. Canned and live music (beat and folk) is employed by 81%.

Seventy-four per cent have rooms available for prayer and counselling, 67% have specific follow-up material available.

There are, inevitably, problems in relationships with local churches – 85% report that the integration of converts into churches is difficult, and 80% complain of lack of support from local churches.

The recurring danger, felt by many, is the 'coffee bar church', though it must be admitted that the inability of local Christians to accept unusual converts increases this tendency.

It would seem from the evidence of music groups and coffee bars that the younger generation of Evangelicals is able and willing to do unorthodox and experimental work in evangelism, particularly among their own generation. In view of the impotence of many churches and ministers in this whole matter, we do well to ask how far young people have any say in the shaping of the programme of their churches, and whether some of their more extreme efforts may not be the direct consequence of the insensitive or disapproving attitudes of older Christians.

20. EVANGELISM-IN-DEPTH

The Evangelical Alliance has, from the start, taken an interest in the strikingly effective Evangelism-in-Depth Campaigns in Latin America, and sponsored the visit to this country of two international leaders of EiD early in 1968. This visit included visits to provincial centres, to the E.A. ministers' conference at Swanwick, and to a meeting of the Commission. Reference is made to this in the final chapter of this Report, but we include here something of the comments made by the visitors and by some of those who have studied EiD. Their report (which follows) gives a significant insight into the way perceptive visitors see the British situation. We are grateful to Dr. Fenton and Mr. Lores for their friendly co-operation in this whole matter.

Findings

'It became evident that there is a felt need in England for an aggressive programme of evangelistic advance at the earliest possible moment. This is not *our* conviction alone; it represents what was said to us in a variety of ways by a great number of people in the course of our visit. And all that we saw and heard during our stay confirmed its validity.

'The great multitudes of England's population are currently untouched by any vital contact with the Gospel of Christ. Only some ten per cent of the population attends church with any regularity, according to D. B. Winter, editor of *Crusade* magazine.

'We have noted a real sense of the inadequacy of previous evangelistic efforts. There is no desire here to minimize anything that the Lord has done through the years, nor to downgrade men and movements that have been obviously blessed by Him. But we sense a widespread disappointment. . . . It is easy to detect a deep conviction, held by many evangelical leaders, that something besides periodic efforts at mass evangelism is needed. If England is to be adequately evangelized, there must be an all-out effort toward the effective mobilization of the whole Church for continuous evangelistic outreach.

'The current crisis in evangelical circles demands a refocusing of our attention on the task of evangelism. It seems to us to be compounded of at least three elements:
(i) The strong separatist emphasis being made in certain quarters today;
(ii) The tendency on the part of some to feel that they can do best by confining their evangelical witness to their own denomination;
(iii) And the fact that there are great numbers of Evangelicals who have no organizational relationship with other Evangelicals and who are left in a state of indecision with regard to such relationships as a result of the conflicting claims that are being heard within the evangelical camp today.

'It is our conviction that in the midst of these tensions and

152

strains, Evangelicals will *not* be held together merely by organizational ties. But there is both historical precedent and scriptural hope for believing that without yielding on basic convictions, Evangelicals who centre on the need of the world for Christ, and their God-given task in His programme of world evangelization, will find ways of standing together in the visible and functional unity which is so desperately needed today.

'It will not be easy to develop and to implement such a programme in England. After our brief visit here, we are not inclined to make light of the tremendous obstacles that churches must confront in undertaking an all-out programme of evangelism. Among these adverse factors would certainly be the following:

'*Current theological trends*, which result in the inability of some denominations to agree even on a definition of evangelism, let alone on ways of carrying out an evangelistic programme. These trends include neo-universalism, the attempt to substitute the changing of the structures of society for the preaching of a gospel of individual conversion, and other deadly and unscriptural emphases with which you are very familiar.

'The relatively *small size of the evangelical community* as compared with the overall population of the country. Any sober evaluation leads one to see that God's people in almost any country are a pathetically small minority in our day, and this is certainly true in England.

'The rapid *urbanization of society*, with consequent difficulties for inner-city churches, further complicates the work of evangelization.

'The *limitations and restrictions placed on mass communications* (especially radio and television) in Great Britain serve to handicap greatly the promotion of evangelical activities and the dissemination of the Gospel itself.

'*Traditional patterns of church activity* often deny priority

153

to evangelism in the church programme. Most churches are more than busy – so busy that the thought of a "new" evangelistic programme seems almost an interruption to regular activities and a burden too great to be borne. The result is that evangelism becomes an "extra", rather than a central part of the church's activity.

'*Unusually heavy pressures on pastors* in these days frequently keep them from the primary function of training the laity for the service of Christ. Every pastor is expected to be an expert in a number of different fields, and frequently his primary task is neglected as a result.

'There is an *attitude of pessimism* and almost of despair in certain circles in the light of the magnitude of the task and the difficulties that are involved in it.

'England is a *highly sophisticated society*, one in which the Christian faith is not a new thing, and where the attitudes of men towards the Gospel seem already almost inflexibly ill-formed.

'It is hardly fair, however, to note only the difficulties without taking full cognizance of the many positive factors which give grounds for hope and faith. Again, the list will necessarily be incomplete, but we should at least note the following elements:

'There is *a great sense of need* for a new and powerful intervention by God. This is openly and freely admitted by many.

'The *wide range of co-operation among Evangelicals* across denominational lines (much wider, incidentally, than that which we find in the United States) gives hope for a united effort such as would be impossible in some other places.

'The *evident blessing of God on recent evangelistic efforts* in Great Britain ought to be of great encouragement to us. Among other things, it has been demonstrated here that evangelicals can unite and that great numbers of people

154

can be reached with the Gospel, even in the midst of the discouraging circumstances of our times.

'The *extraordinary variety of evangelistic efforts* already being carried on here, with some measure of success, should be a cause of real encouragement. We have been much impressed with what is being done in different areas of England along the lines of telephone counselling, coffee-bar evangelism, university missions, visitation programmes, industrial evangelism, youth movements, especially in the schools, and abundant evangelistic and theological literature.

'Among England's other remarkable resources are the great number of full-time evangelists in this country. We are told that there may be as many as two hundred of these men and that a goodly group of them met together some months ago to discuss their mutual interests.

'It should be noted in this connection that Evangelism-in-Depth, rightly understood and implemented, increases the need for professional evangelists and very frequently increases their usefulness as well. It is sometimes thought that the great stress in Evangelism-in-Depth on the mobilization of every believer may serve to leave the evangelists jobless. The very opposite result has been our experience in Latin America. Without minimizing the importance and essential nature of the witness of individual Christians, we have seen opportunities for mass evangelism, using men with special evangelistic gifts, greatly multiplied. The fact that there is a "work force" available for this sort of thing in Great Britain should be a source of great encouragement.

'We recognize that there is considerable difference of opinion among British Evangelicals as to the feasibility of an Evangelism-in-Depth type programme for your country. We have had contact with quite a variety of these viewpoints, and at the risk of over-simplification we might group these various attitudes under three main headings:

'These are those who are completely negative. Here is no

155

denial of the blessing of God in Latin America and elsewhere but a strong feeling that conditions peculiar to England, including the impossibility of denominational support for such a programme, financial and leadership problems, theological orientation which does not allow for this type of evangelism, etc., make Evangelism-in-Depth unsuitable for use in this country.

'Among some, there is a real openness to the possibility of some adaptation of Evangelism-in-Depth, but with serious reservations:

'(i) The unusual difficulties involved in interdenominational co-operation in Great Britain.

'(ii) The mobilizing of the entire constituency of any great number of local churches in Great Britain seems to some almost impossible.

'(iii) The warm spiritual climate which characterizes Latin American evangelicals is almost non-existent in England.

'In many quarters, we found a highly favourable reaction to Evangelism-in-Depth. Wide recognition of the scriptural and practical validity of the principles of Evangelism-in-Depth has been manifested by many Evangelicals here. Moreover, we have seen evidence that most or all of these principles have already been successfully implemented in certain local churches in Great Britain. Remarkable success has been attained in isolated instances in the mobilization and training of church members for effective witness, in the carrying on of visitation evangelism programmes, and in the utilization of other methods solidly based on the principles which are at the heart of Evangelism-in-Depth.

'Moreover, among these people who look favourably upon the use of an Evangelism-in-Depth type approach in England there is an increasing recognition that present moods, however useful, are inadequate in Britain to be coordinated for a more effective carrying out of the task of evangelism.

'We find some element of truth in all the positions expressed above. We would not deny the difficulties involved in the implementation of such a programme in England; we would remind ourselves, and our English brethren, that a strong element of the miraculous will have to characterize any effective programme of evangelistic advance. By every human standard, the difficulties have been insuperable in every situation that Evangelism-in-Depth has faced so far in other parts of the world. God's people are in a minority; they are sorely divided; their resources of leadership and personnel seem terribly limited; the "atmosphere" is not always right for advance; evangelicals, even in the young, growing churches, are often dull, apathetic, and in desperate need of revival.

'The fact of the matter is that if the Gospel is to make any significant advance in *any* part of the world today, a miracle will have to be involved. And while there is a sense in which miracles are purely acts of sovereign grace, there is plenty of evidence, both in Scripture and in present-day history, that such miracles begin to take place when God's people (perhaps in very small numbers at first) count on Him to bring them to pass, in the midst of the most difficult circumstances.

'We began by stating our conviction that Britain needs an all-out programme of evangelism. It would seem to us that Britain needs the type of programme that will be based, to the fullest possible extent, on those scriptural presuppositions and principles which are embodied in the Evangelism-in-Depth strategy.

'This is not to say that it is essential to use the name "Evangelism-in-Depth", or that the programme must closely resemble that which has been carried on in Latin America.

'Indeed, there would have to be many modifications, some of which even we, on the basis of our brief contact with the

157

British evangelical scene, can foresee. With perhaps one or two exceptions, it would not be possible to secure the support of whole denominations in England, as had been done in Latin America. It is much more likely that the project could be effectively carried out in England by basing it on the local churches, the local evangelical councils, and the larger groupings such as the Evengelical Alliance and other groups having similar interests. Moreover, it is probable that in England the approach should be on a regional basis, to begin with, rather than on a national one. It may well be that a pilot programme, based on an even smaller geographical entity than a region, may be needed.

'But all these are details – important and significant, but secondary in the light of the following questions: Are British Evangelicals open to whatever new approach the Lord has for them, whatever the source of that approach and whatever difficulties may lie in the way of it? Are they convinced that it is the will of God that every believer is meant to have a part in the task of evangelization, and that we are not likely to make significant progress in this task until we utilize every legitimate means, both spiritual and material, to bring about that mobilization? Is it possible that we can learn some things from the experience of our brethren in other parts of the world, and are we willing to study what has happened there, to learn whatever lessons God may have for us? Is there not a possibility that if God's frustrated, burdened, almost despairing people will trust Him for some fresh manifestation of His power, He may give it, making His strength perfect in our weakness, and confounding once again the enemies of His Gospel? Is it outside the bounds of our eschatology and of our belief in God to expect that in these last days He may yet enable His church to make a mighty evangelistic impact on the world, and particularly on our homelands?'

A careful assessment of EiD was made for the Commission by one of its members. After outlining the way in which it has worked in Latin America, the writer makes the following comments about the situation as compared with Britain.

EiD's development is in the realm of the under-developed world, the world of the illiterate, the poor, and the downtrodden. In the main they are dealing with urban workers with a very low standard of living, though they are aware of a gradual awakening to the outside world largely stimulated by the appearance of transistor radios.

The emotional temperament of the Latin American is very different from that of the West European. Their stress on the work of the Holy Spirit and prayer has very special overtones unrelated to our own culture.

The Latin American is ostentatious. The whole idea of parade and procession is very popular. (This was much used in the sixteenth century by Roman Catholics, when many conversions took place.)

There is also an emphasis on the spirit of leadership distinct from our own background and with it the whole cult of personal contact and influence. This seems to bear overtones in Latin America which we do not know about in this country. This may be related to the revolutionary spirit evident in Latin America.

Relationships between Protestants and Catholics have dramatically altered within the last decade. EiD has taken advantage of the results of Vatican Council II. They have come in at a crucial moment. The situation Protestant-wise is very different from that of our own nation. No one is called 'Protestant' in Latin America, but 'evangelical', which to them is equated with the Protestant faith, due to the background of Christian missions. There is less Liberalism amongst Protestants there than in this country, and this means that the possibility of relationships is different.

Dr. Fenton and Mr. Lores made a number of recommendations which were considered by the Commission, and which have been partially incorporated into the final section of this Report. Some of these recommendations are in abeyance pending the publication of this Report and the discussion which will follow.

21. GENERAL SUMMARY

The compiling and arranging of the information contained in the preceding section has, in itself, provided an unusual picture of the variety as well as the scale of evangelistic enterprise. In the evangelical world with which we have largely been concerned, there is no lack of enterprise or willingness to tackle new situations; there is certainly a consistent concern to bring others to know Jesus Christ and to make His Gospel known as widely as possible.

Nevertheless there are certain tendencies which give reason for feeling that this basic enthusiasm is not getting anything like its proper reward.

There is the tendency for organizations and individuals to operate outside the churches, or in a very loose connection with them. This may well be because of the innate conservatism of the churches, which are unable to act enterprisingly because of the drag created by power in the hands of elderly members and by an undiscriminating conservatism. It must be remembered that one rôle of the Church is to express its members' dependence upon God, and to give them a sense of security in a world of flux. It is only a short step from this to the assumption that everything about the Church must remain the same; change or novelty are *very* hard to tolerate. Yet it is clear that without a close relationship and involvement in the life of the churches, all evangelism is in difficulties, especially in caring for any 'converts'.

Another tendency is for Evangelicals to act pragmatically, not working to a planned long-term strategy. In the matter of radio, for instance, most think of getting their minister on the air for a Sunday service when they would do better to get one of their young men in a trainee producer's job inside the BBC organization. A need suddenly arises – drug addiction, for example – and suddenly there is a rash of movements, books and rallies dealing with this theme. This kind of thing results in a number of unco-ordinated parallel organizations, each with office, magazine, mailing list, advertising schedule, committee, board of referees, and so on. Again problems are created in relation to the churches who are called upon to support these worthy causes.

Ideally, the necessary co-ordination of these multifarious activities must come from one body to which sufficient respect and responsibility is given by most, if not all, Evangelicals engaged in evangelism. However, in the absence of such a body and the unlikelihood of its inception in the near future, we urge that mutual information and consultation take place wherever possible. The Evangelical Alliance is the obvious channel and we ask its Council to consider extending the facilities in this field. This will demand confidence and co-operation, as well as financial support, from those taking advantage of the service.

Chapter Four

MENDING THE NETS

Conclusions and Recommendations of the
Commission

The task of evangelizing Britain is not simple, but
complex. It must be attacked at many points if the situation is to be changed. There is a constant peril of seeking
immediate solutions and easy options. Though modern
society uses many 'instant' products, no single method will
provide instant evangelism. Our investigations emphasize
that evangelism is not so much a programme, more a way
of life. Attitudes need to be fostered. Groups need to be
reached. Methods need to be considered. Units need to be
mobilized. Rôles need to be defined. (The discerning reader
of the earlier sections of this Report will have noted implicit
comment on many aspects of evangelism; this final section
selects and emphasizes some of the more important conclusions only.)

22. ATTITUDES TO BE FOSTERED

Rather than plunge straight into recommending particular courses of action, we begin by stating our considered
opinion that the fundamental need of our day is a change
of attitude among Christians. To be quite specific, Evangelicals need to re-think the implications of our Lord's
command to 'go into all the world'. Traditional interpretation has taken this in a strictly geographical sense. However, Christians may be 'distributed' very widely, and still

live in a world of their own. Our attitude to 'worldliness', for example, has bred a ghetto mentality. We need to break out of this in two ways:

a. *Into the Cultural World*. England is a mission field, and this involves us in the disciplined study of contemporary language and the thought-forms behind it, particularly as used by the mass media. There is a cultural gap between the Church and the world around it, aggravated by the predominance in it of middle-class members. We are at once out of touch with both the intellectual opinion-formers and the 'workers'.

We recommend the establishment of a Christian Communication Centre in this country, to provide a cultural meeting-point where interested Evangelicals can explore together the disciplines of art, music, drama, literature, etc. It is hoped that this would open the way for genuine dialogue as defined earlier in the Report. On the one hand, Christians could listen to the world and interpret its thoughts and feelings to the Church. On the other hand, Christians with the necessary gifts could learn to speak to the world in an idiom it understood. For example, we believe that radio and television would be much more available for witness if material of the right quality could be provided.

National and local broadcasting would not be the only fruitful outlet for evangelical programmes in the current idiom. Video tape recorders will soon be produced at reasonable cost, and are likely to be a major technological development in the educational field. These units make possible the visual play-back of video-tape cassettes through a normal television receiver. The application for evangelism is obvious. For example, small house groups could invite neighbours to watch a first-class presentation of some aspect of the Christian faith or life, with a view to discussing it afterwards. Illustrated Bible teaching could be made widely available in a form that has many advantages over the present tape recording. Furthermore, local amateur groups could be encouraged to produce their own visual programmes. From this field would develop some of the talent needed by the national services. We hope that the churches will explore and exploit this medium as soon as it is available.

b. *Into the Communal World*. We do not see any great improvement in Christian witness until individual believers are much more deeply involved in the life of society and in a better position to have real relationships with people for other than spiritual purposes. We may need to learn all over again what it means to be a 'friend of sinners'. This cannot be organized, and basically depends on the individual believer's response to this statement and initiative in applying it. In later sections we shall indicate how churches and ministers could encourage this, but perhaps a few practical illustrations at this stage will help.

Christians in industry should accept involvement with trade unions, sports clubs, welfare services, etc. Unless clearly called out, they should stay in the situations in which God called them, believing that He needs witnesses where they are. Christians should also seek practical guidance as to where they live, whether to stay in the inner city belt or to move to another area where there is no witness. In any case, top priority should be given to making as many non-Christian friends as possible within the immediate neighbourhood. This will probably involve some community service of a voluntary kind, which must be undertaken for its own sake and not as an evangelistic gimmick. We would also mention the difficulty of building effective bridges into the Church if Christians travel many miles away to worship in a 'good' fellowship under a 'sound' minister.

The real tragedy is that most believers start the Christian life with many unbelieving friends, but this circle is gradually reduced until there are few. Matthew gives us a scriptural precedent for maintaining former social links. Our studies lead us to believe that personal friendship is still and probably always will be the primary means of leading others to Christ.

23. GROUPS TO BE REACHED

Christianity started with a group of adults rather than children, men rather than women, workers rather than scholars. If our statistics are representative, the evangelical force today is almost exactly the opposite. The situation cries out for a re-focusing of our objectives and a re-deployment of our resources.

a. *Adults*. Much concentrated effort has gone into work among children and young people. Often our best Christians are swallowed up in this section of our work. We believe the time has come to restore a proper balance by using some of our best talent in an all-out attempt to reach adults, particularly between twenty and forty. It may once have been true that parents could be reached through their children; we believe the stress now should be that we will reach the children if we get their parents. Family worship and all-age instruction have shown the advantage of including the parents in the planning.

b. *Men*. The absence of men, both from our churches and in the fruits of evangelistic activity, is very striking. Admittedly, they represent the most difficult segment of our society to reach with the Gospel, but this ought not to divert us into apparently 'easier' work. The churches must make an urgent effort to convert men. How can this be done? It is difficult to bring a man out of his home at night after a day's work away from home or away from the car and garden at the week-end. The opportunity to reach him at work is limited. The key is obviously personal befriending by a believer with an opportunity to meet him informally. Mutual hospitality may be the next stage, and we would underline the advantage of approaching married couples *as couples* and seeking to win them together as a unit.

c. *'Working Class'*. Our analysis of some thousands of conversions from a sociological point of view was profoundly disturbing. There were nearly four times more than the national population average in the upper two groups. In the other three groups, which together comprise the majority of our fellow-countrymen, there were less than half. We have tried to identify some of the factors leading to the disproportion. The general background of our ministers, and the academic training which has moulded them; the traditional dress, music, and language in our services; our appeal to the intellect and our neglect of the emotions; our reliance upon dedicated natural gifts rather than supernatural gifts supplied by One who is no respecter of persons – these and many other factors have been mentioned in our discussions. Our time and talents have been too limited to investigate this whole issue at depth and we would express the hope that a Christian sociologist might be led to examine the whole situation very thoroughly and produce a critical analysis of our failure here.

d. *Youth*. Undoubtedly this group is the easiest 'target' for our evangelism. Relatively uncommitted, idealistic, still in the most formative period of life, prone to meet in groups which can be contacted – young people are open to our approaches, as the numerical attendance at Christian coffee bars shows. But there is another side to the picture, and we urge all youth evangelists to give special attention to two major problems.

The first is that of stability. In these days when young people are looking for a meaningful experience centred in the emotions rather than the thoughts, it is absolutely essential not to expect or ask for a decision until the rational content of the Gospel has been clearly grasped. Existential experiment with a new kind of religious experience is not a response to the Gospel and will not lead to a continuing Christian life.

The second problem is that of integration. Most of our churches are quite different in atmosphere from the context in which a decision was registered, and must be ready to make allowance and adjustment for an influx of youngsters with little or no experience of church behaviour patterns. It may be that an intermediary stage of fellowship will have to be planned as a 'halfway house'.

24. METHODS TO BE CONSIDERED

We want to stress the importance of starting with the Gospel and what it implies about people before examining a particular method of evangelism. The truth we proclaim cannot be detached from the 'format' in which we proclaim it. Any technique must be theologically valid as well as psychologically sound. In this section, however, we are commenting on two approaches from a practical point of view. The first is familiar to us and has been the most publicised outreach during the last few years, namely, the large crusade centred upon one evangelist. The other is known only by repute and many are asking whether it provides the answer to our need – namely, 'Evangelism-in-Depth' as practised in Latin America and, in other versions, in Nigeria and elsewhere.

a. *Crusades*. There is no doubt that many have come to a faith in the Lord Jesus Christ through this channel and not a few of them have gone further into full-time Christian service. Denominational differences have been overcome as Christians have united in these projects, and many churches have been spiritually quickened. Christianity has been made a talking-point, and people have heard the Gospel who would not have entered a church. On the other hand, we must get a true perspective and recognize that crusades account for only a small percentage of all conversions taking place.

We doubt whether this pattern will be as prominent in the seventies. Our questionnaires and interviews – in common with Press and similar reports – reveal a declining confidence among the churches and ministers in this method. The expressed dissatisfaction centres in the inadequate understanding of the inquirer about the nature of the appeal and the limited counselling given afterwards. This seems particularly true of those responding in their early 'teens. As an immediate suggestion, we suggest that evangelists should seek other ways of challenging youngsters of fifteen and under.

It is also clear that the further a crusade is removed from the life of the local churches, the more acute is the problem of continuity and integration. This is accentuated when the invitation to an evangelist does not come from the local churches but from interested individuals. There are difficulties, too, within the crusade meetings themselves. It is very doubtful if many outsiders can be taken from a position of complete ignorance to full faith in Christ within the compass of one rally. This may explain why so many of the inquirers showing lasting results come from a church background or association. Furthermore, the limited time and stereotyped method of the counselling seems inadequate to ascertain the personal position and needs of the individual.

In the light of these difficulties, we would like to make two suggestions for future crusades. First, we would like to see a shift in emphasis from the inspirational to the instructional content in the crusade meetings themselves. We understand the gift of the evangelist to be primarily the ability to make Gospel truth clear to the unbeliever. In these days 'Gospel preaching' must include apologetics as well as salvation, statements about God as well as about Christ, the foundation of creation on which redemption is based, the demand of the law as well as the offer of the Gospel, the significance of the resurrection as well as the death of our Lord. We believe that there is considerable scope for such teaching missions to the unbeliever, particularly among men, who are deeply suspicious of emotional pressure.

Second, we ask that the traditional methods of appeal and counselling be re-considered in the light of Scripture and our contemporary situation, and that evangelists be ready to modify their techniques at this point. It may even be better in the long run not to have an open appeal within the meeting, and to invite those who seriously desire to go further to contact a counsellor (suitably identified) at the exits or, better still, to leave their name and address so that a trained counsellor can contact them at home and spend the necessary time to discover their real response. This, of course, would demand real co-operation at local church level, but we question whether an area crusade ought to be held if this is lacking.

b. *Evangelism-in-Depth*. This concept has attracted increasing interest, partly because of the spectacular results. Christians in England must be willing to learn from their brethren overseas, particularly in the younger and more vigorous churches. We have studied the principles and practice in some detail and come to the following conclusions.

On the one hand, we have found much that is helpful and necessary for our future strategy in this country. Kenneth Strachan's basic theorem seems to us unassailable: 'The growth of any movement is in direct proportion to the success of that movement in mobilizing its total membership for the propagation of its beliefs.' This is not new (in the light of Acts 8.4!), but it is true – as is the converse, that decline will follow the failure to do this. In putting the fundamental responsibility on to the individual believer, assisted by pastors and evangelists, we feel this strategy has laid a sound foundation. The mobilization of all resources of the church and the penetration of all levels of society are also vital insights.

On the other hand, one vital feature of EiD, the simultaneous programme on a national basis, raises other questions. After careful consideration, we do not believe this to be feasible under our present conditions. The mixed theological character of the mainline denominations, the scattered and sometimes divided evangelical force, the non-availability of mass media for direct evangelistic broadcasting, the sophistication of our society and reserve of our national temperament and, above all, the current pessimism among believers – all these factors militate against a fullscale application of Latin American methods to our country.

It would be possible, however, and desirable, to apply many of their discoveries to evangelism at the local and district level. Where there are a sufficient number of Evangelicals in proper relationship with one another this could be done. We recommend that EiD handbooks be made freely available in such situations. It would be an added advantage if the material could be condensed and adapted for English readers.

25. UNITS TO BE MOBILIZED

We have tried to focus our attention on the basic units likely to be used in evangelizing this nation over the next few years. At the risk of being misunderstood, we state our opinion that the denominations and ecumenical groupings are not likely to fulfil this rôle until a much greater consistency in understanding both the message and the mission is reached. We believe the future lies with those units which make for local, direct, and personal methods. Among others, three stand out as supremely important – namely, the church, the cell, and the home.

a. *Church.* By this we mean the local fellowship of believers sharing the same worship, fellowship, leadership, and discipline. While we recognize that scripturally we ought only to have one such church in each place, it must be acknowledged that this rarely applies in England today; until it does, we must use the churches that do exist as the channel for our outreach. In some cases, co-operation between churches will be possible on the lines indicated in Chapter 2 of this Report.

There will need to be conscious definition of objectives and bold redirection of resources if the local church is to be effective. Activities will need to meet specific and basic needs to justify their existence. More time and money will need to be spent on outreach, which means correspondingly less on other things. Children's work may need to have less emphasis, so that adults' might have more. Above all, total demands on the members for direct church work must be reduced in order to release them among unbelievers (for example, in cells and homes, and in the general life of the community). Of course, there must be maintained that warm Christian fellowship which is the vital background and base for all evangelism. But this may be better fostered by programmes for the whole church rather than through a multiplicity of departments and organizations, each of which demands its own officers and committees.

We need 'mission churches' rather than church missions, programmes geared to continuous evangelism rather than spasmodic forays into the 'outside'. We cannot rely on constant invitations to 'come' to church, but must learn to 'go' out all the time. Of course, members will need training, but we emphasize that this should be intensely practical with a lot of 'field' work, rather than just a series of talks (or tapes!) on the subject.

We would like to see available to churches a team of consultants who could be called in to spend enough time

171

with a church to help its minister, leaders, and members to evaluate its real impact on the community around it. We believe that such consultants, whose support would need to be found by the church, would be of invaluable help because of their objective approach and wider knowledge. They could make suggestions for better re-deployment of resources and greater efficiency in evangelism without the inhibitions of being personally involved in the situation. It is likely that both Anglican and Free Church specialists would be needed, in view of the different character of the two types of organization; while pastoral experience would be necessary, it would be essential to have some able laymen available.

b. *Cell*. Cellular structure and multiplication by division are biological patterns which seem to have an application to spiritual life. We consider the small group to be one of the most potent factors in evangelism today, primarily because it makes possible real personal relationships and genuine conversation. Cells are very adaptable and may be developed in professional, cultural and social settings. Free from the institutional church and its bad public image, mostly led by laymen rather than the clergy, and 'off the premises', such cells encourage both believers and unbelievers to be vocal.

Certain dangers need to be avoided. Cells must not become 'meetings'. They can be introverted and become a means of isolating believers from their environment (as has happened to a number of cells in factories, for example). A clique will lose its capacity for reproduction. In extreme cases, a cell can become a divisive body within a church, or even claim to be a church itself.

The difficulties, however, are a measure of the potential, and we believe this method should be exploited to the full. Because they represent growing-points of life, cells often appear (and disappear) quite spontaneously. However, they can be encouraged, and some training could be given to potential leaders. There is room for a handbook on the subject, which would share existing experience.

c. *Home.* Our investigations lead us to emphasize this unit, which is so often taken for granted. We are not now referring to meetings held in homes, but to the informal practice of hospitality, particularly to strangers. The New Testament clearly lays this duty and privilege on believers. This kind of witness has particular value towards those who have never known a Christian home and who may find the atmosphere one of the most impressive demonstrations of the faith, whether during a brief visit or an extended stay.

There is an art of hospitality which Christians will need to learn. A genuine love for people *as people* and an interest in other than spiritual subjects are vital qualifications. Differences of social habit (for example, in smoking and drinking) must be faced. Time and trouble must be taken in the skills of courtesy and hospitality.

26. RÔLES TO BE DEFINED

Certain key figures have emerged in our discussions and we have tried to crystallize the pattern of their contribution to the total evangelistic strategy.

a. *Evangelist.* While the responsibility for evangelism is undoubtedly placed on the whole Church, we recognize the special gift to the Church of the office of evangelist. In the New Testament there is very little information about the specific nature of his calling, but clearly his prime responsibility is to relate the Gospel to the unbeliever and the unbeliever to the Saviour. Over the last one hundred years this function has been increasingly exercised in a way which has emphasized the public rather than the personal, and reaping rather than sowing. This pattern owes much to American revivalism; with it has come a relative independence from church structures, and latterly the appearance of organizations gathered around one or more evangelists.

We are concerned about the degree of mutual suspicion between pastors and evangelists, perhaps due to the degree of separation between their ministries and consequent lack of understanding. Mutual embarrassment can thus be caused. For example, the problems of inter-church co-operation are much more acute for the pastor who stays in a locality for some years than for the evangelist who visits briefly and feels free to have anyone on his platform while he retains the preaching office. We believe that one of the urgent needs is a much closer relationship between evangelists and the churches and suggest four areas in which this could be explored.

First, in *recognition*. If an evangelist is seen as a gift of the ascended Lord to His Church, as is a pastor, his call from the Lord should be confirmed by the church in which he is in membership. He should be set apart for his ministry in the church and maintain links with it during his itinerancy. He may develop a 'Council of Reference' consisting of churches in which he has worked (rather than a list of individuals, which seems more usual at present). It may be possible to seek the recognition of larger groups of churches, even denominations, and this ought to be obtained wherever possible. This approach would seem to us preferable to setting up organizations and societies independent of the churches.

Second, in *support*. It has become clear to us that many evangelists in this country are inadequately supported. This involves some in part-time employment, others in too many 'one-night stands', and a few in ministry outside this country for part of the year. With the greater recognition outlined above would come the responsibility of the churches to carry this burden for those whom they have set apart. This would bring about a much closer relationship in what Paul describes as the fellowship of giving and receiving.

Third, in *integration*. We would like to see evangelists working on the basis of more time and less space for each project. An evangelist attached to a local church or group of churches for a period of some months could be greatly used to exploit the fringes and extend the frontiers. To do this he will need to give much more time to personal work and less to the platform, more to the smaller groups and less to the large audience.

Fourth, in *training*. Evangelists could fulfil a vital rôle in training church members by taking them into secular situations and showing them how to make contact. In this way, young Christians with the potential gift of an evangelist would be detected and developed.

One final recommendation we would like to make under this heading will be new to most churches in this country, though familiar on the mission field. We urge churches to revive the 'evangelist' as an office *in the local fellowship*. We believe this to be true to Scripture. Whether part-time or full-time, someone with the necessary qualifications and experience could be set apart (perhaps with the laying-on of hands) and regarded as a member of the team with the minister and other leaders. His main function would be to lead the church in its outreach, break fresh ground for the members to exploit, and do personal work among the unbelievers contacted.

b. *Minister*. A basic difficulty arises because of the different church structures in the New Testament and today. In theory, the minister's function is directed towards the flock; he has been called, equipped, and ordained for pastoral rather than evangelistic service. But our churches tend to revolve around one man, and his interests and activities are inevitably reflected in the congregation. He is therefore in a key rôle when it comes to evangelism, and he may well have to 'do the work of an evangelist' if his church members are to be encouraged to do so. There are four ways in which he may do this, without turning the worship services into miniature crusades!

First, he must *share*. To keep all the initiative and control in his own hands will create a passive congregation which is likely to be inactive outside the church as well as inside. If he can work out the principle of the priesthood of all believers *within* the church, in conducting worship as well as other meetings, he is more likely to encourage the active involvement in witness of all believers outside the church. The emphasis must be on team-work, and involves departure from that dichotomy between clergy and laity which has caused 'layman' to become a synonym for 'amateur'.

Second, he must *train*. His teaching ministry is to equip the saints for their work of ministry in the world. Two branches of education are needed. On the one hand is the formal instruction and systematic exposition of the whole counsel of God. One service each Sunday could well be centred on this and would have profound effects, particularly on the men of the congregation. On the other hand, there must be informal learning in which participation and application are the main thrusts. The minister may organize this, but is probably wise not to become directly involved unless he and his members can forget that he is the minister.

Third, he must *release*. This involves resisting the temptation to saddle every promising member with an office in the church. The problem is that churches develop an elaborate machinery which swallows all available personnel. From his position the minister can encourage the church to give some of its key workers time for evangelism. The suggestion relating to consultants is relevant here and could give vital backing to a minister.

Fourth, he must *lead*. Although he may not be equipped

176

for evangelism, he must recognize that his attitudes will be a powerful influence in the church. He can offer both encouragement and an example, particularly if he is seen to be keen on personal work. His participation in house-to-house visitation (perhaps minus clerical collar) would be a real stimulus to others.

As churches are shaped by ministers, ministers are shaped by colleges. We urge those responsible for their training to make sure that the curriculum includes a thorough introduction to the contemporary world, cultural and communal, in addition to a thorough grounding in the Word. The behavioural sciences must be given more attention. Training in modern communication is essential. Above all, we believe that there must be greater variety in training, with much less emphasis on academic qualifications for those whose personality, background, and contribution would be handicapped by being pressed into an intellectual mould. We are glad to hear that some colleges are already aware of these needs and are diversifying their courses.

c. *Believer*. In the last analysis, we believe that the individual believer is the key figure in all future evangelism. The Great Commission comes through the apostles to all disciples. Only as all believers are mobilized for this task will the cause of the Gospel prosper in Britain. We cannot avoid this simple fact. We have already spoken about the need for Christians to be more involved in their society in such a way as to make possible genuine personal relationships with those they seek to win. Two other comments may be added at this point.

First, believers must use their *lips*. No one ever heard the Gospel unless someone spoke about it. Yet breaking the sound-barrier and opening the lips of silent saints seems an insuperable task. Why do believers find it so difficult to talk naturally about their Lord? Fear of being regarded as peculiar, disappointment over misunderstood witnessing,

177

over-intellectualized concepts of the Faith not easily communicated, social inhibitions about discussing 'private' matters like religion – these and many other reasons can be given.

But what is the remedy? We believe that one great step forward would be made if opportunities could be created within the church for believers to speak freely about the Lord with one another. If we cannot talk about Him to those who are sympathetic because they also know Him, we are not likely to mention Him among the indifferent or hostile. Further, it must be stressed that we do not need to know a great deal of theology or apologetics before we can witness to our faith. A simple, honest and real testimony to Christ is often highly effective and answers many questions. Some of our more elaborate 'training schemes' for evangelism and counselling may have the paradoxical effect of frightening away Christians who conclude that it is too difficult for the ordinary believer.

Second, believers must use their *lives*. Consistent discipleship is our authority to speak. Christians are not likely to commend their Saviour unless their walk with Him is deepening every day. We make an urgent appeal to all readers of this Report to examine themselves at this point and make quite sure that their affections, thoughts, and motives are rooted in Him who died, rose, and is coming again for us. Earlier in these pages we quoted the opinion that the Church has no problem of communication, it is conveying only too clearly what it is. There is enough truth in this observation to justify the view that the major handicap to evangelism is the shallow relationship many Christians have with their Lord and their unwillingness to know Him so deeply as to share His sufferings and enjoy the power of His resurrection. We do not need to wait for 'revival' to put this right. Perhaps we should be praying for repentance more than anything else.

27. CONCLUSION

If it was hoped that this Commission would produce a blueprint of evangelism which would miraculously transform the situation, many will be disappointed. We have sought to be realistic and face the facts, rejecting the modern desire for immediate solutions which has infected Christian thinking. But we would take up one contemporary idea – 'Do-It-Yourself'. The time has gone for 'vicarious' evangelism in which Christians seek to transfer their own responsibility either to professionals or even to the impersonal method (read *The Gospel Blimp*[1] for a devastating exposure of this kind of thinking). Personal evangelism is still the prime method and the hope of this Commission is that this will be stimulated by the reading of the Report.[2]

We have naturally concentrated our work on the human factors, but we have been mindful all the way through that the battle is supernatural. 'On the other side' of the battle-field are ranged the spiritual hosts of wickedness in heavenly places, whose subtle power and opposition will always be encountered when the Church leaves its sheltered position and challenges Satan's kingdom. This is the basic reason why there is no easy option.

We must be realists, but there is no need to be defeatists. As we move into the seventies, we remember that they are years of grace, years of our Lord. The decisive conflict with evil has already been fought and won on the Cross and in the tomb. Jesus has been given all authority in heaven and on earth and in His Name we fulfil our ambassadorial responsibility.

1. *The Gospel Blimp*, by Joe Bayly (Victory Press).
2. See (e.g.) *Personal Evangelism*, by H. C. Pawson (Epworth).

Appendix

STATISTICAL SURVEY

The Commission was anxious to obtain reliable information about the relative effectiveness of different means of evangelism. A group of statisticians was consulted, and the method decided upon was to select a broad group of Christians now in membership of evangelical churches and find out how they were brought to a living faith in Jesus Christ.

Mr. David Longley (now working in Nigeria with the Wycliffe Bible Translators) planned and carried through a survey in the course of which some 5,000 Christians were interviewed and questionnaires completed. The initial sorting of the returned questionnaires and the decision to use a computer for analysing help was done by Dr. David Shoesmith, then of the Schools Council. When he moved to Cambridge, the task of assessing the results and writing this report fell to Mr. Peter Brierley, working on surveys in the Ministry of Defence.

In this Report we offer only the Summary of the Main Findings of this Survey. Very much more information was generated by the Survey, of course, and this will be published separately.

This Survey is limited to England only. In our 'Findings' we use the word 'Christian' to denote those who were interviewed, and 'conversion' relates to a specific 'experience' of turning to Christ. A 'definite' conversion here simply means one which took place at a specific and recollected time.

It would be impossible to mention by name all those who

have helped in numerous ways in the preparation of this report. But special mention must be made of Dr. Colin Day of the Computer Centre who gave a tremendous amount of time and computer expertise in writing programmes which gave answers in a remarkably short time. Our thanks also go to Miss Ann Quilliam of the CPAS who did a large amount of form coding for us.

SUMMARY OF MAIN FINDINGS

Comparison with National Figures of Population

1. The proportion of Christians in the higher social classes is more than double the national figure, and the proportion in the lower groups about one-third.

2. The proportion of English male Christians is less than the proportion of males in England, but not greatly less.

3. English Christians live predominantly in the south of England.

Definiteness of Conversion

1. Two out of every three Christians can specify the actual day of conversion.

2. The proportion of definite conversions increased slightly between 1920 and 1960.

Means of Conversion

1. Three out of every ten having a definite experience of conversion were converted in the context of a church.

2. The proportion of conversions in a church context appears to move in a 15 year cycle of peak and subsequent decline.

3. The proportion of conversions through a professional evangelist has markedly increased since 1949.

4. The means of conversion for professional people differed from those in other economic groups.

Past Influence

1. The influence of the home leads to one conversion in every four.

2. Personal witness outside the home leads additionally to one conversion in every four.

3. The influence of the home has been declining steadily since 1920, and rapidly since 1950.

4. The influence of those outside the home has been steadily rising since 1920.

5. 'Internal sensations' influence those in the lower occupational groups more than others.

Age of Conversion

1. Three in every four are converted under the age of 20, and one in every six under the age of 12.

2. Of those converted over the age of 20, about half are married.

3. The older a person, the more likely he/she is to be converted in a church context or alone or reading the Bible.

4. The older a person the greater the influence of personal witness and 'internal sensations', and the less the influence of the home.

5. The average age of those converted under the age of 20 since 1960 was $14\frac{3}{4}$ years. It was a little less for those coming from a Christian home.

6. The average age of conversion for those converted under the age of 20 has been increasing slightly since 1960.

Place of Conversion

1. Three in every four are converted in their home area.

2. One in every ten is converted at a camp, conference, etc.

3. Eleven in every 20 teenagers are converted at a camp, conference, etc.

4. The means of conversion and past influence varied from one part of the country to another.

Home Background

1. Half of those converted come from a Christian home.

2. Four-fifths of those converted under the age of 12 come from a Christian home.

3. The proportion of men and women converted coming from a Christian home is approximately equal.

4. Only one in three of those converted when married came from a Christian home.

Church Attendance

1. Seven in every ten of those converted attended church regularly before their conversion.

2. One in every four who were converted but did not come from a Christian home attended church regularly before conversion.

3. The proportion of those converted attending church regularly before conversion has been steadily declining since 1900.

4. Past influences leading to conversion differed according to whether a person was regular or not regular in church attendance before conversion.

5. Of every 20 converted attending church regularly before conversion, nine were men and eleven women.

We append four of the charts and diagrams from the full Statistical Report, for interest and as a 'sample' of the material gathered by the group. The interpretation of these apart from the full Report is, however, likely to be unreliable.

Fig. 5 *Means of conversion and major past influences leading to conversion.*

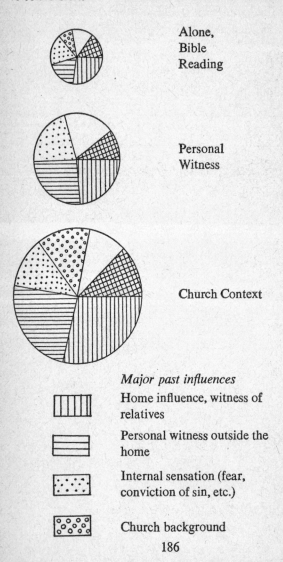

Alone,
Bible
Reading

Personal
Witness

Church Context

Major past influences

Home influence, witness of
relatives

Personal witness outside the
home

Internal sensation (fear,
conviction of sin, etc.)

Church background

The size of the circles represents the proportion in each category.

Regular
Youth Work

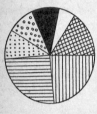

Spasmodic Efforts

Professional
Evangelist

Film

Radio,
Literature

Christian teaching in youth
outside the church

Other past influences

Past influence unknown or
not answered

Fig 13 *Percentage of definite conversions which were influenced by the witness of a home or relatives quinquennially since 1899.*

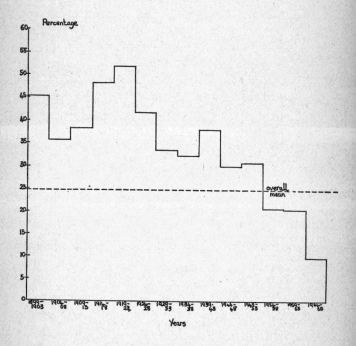

Fig. 14 *Percentage of definite conversions which were influenced through personal witness outside the home quinquennially since 1899.*

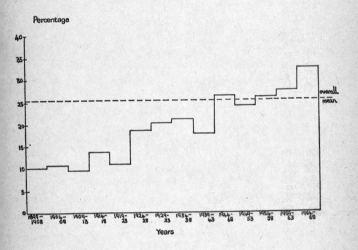

Fig. 19 *Age of conversion by means of conversion*

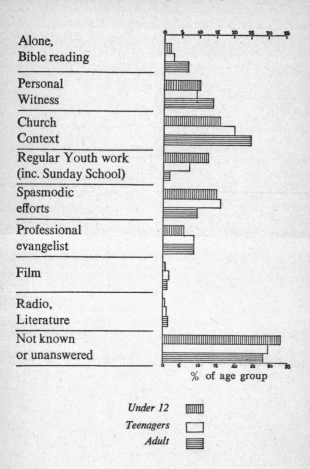

% of age group

Under 12
Teenagers
Adult